Teachings of

ZEN

Compiled and translated by

Thomas Cleary

Shambhala

Boston & London 1998

Shambhala Publications, Inc.
Horticultural Hall
300 Massachusetts Avenue
Boston, Massachusetts 02115

http://www.shambhala.com

8 7 6 5 4 3 2 1

First Edition

Printed in Canada

Book design by Wesley B. Tanner / Passim Editions

⊗ This edition is printed on acid-free paper that meets the
American National Standards Institute Z39.48

Distributed in the United States by Random House, Inc.,
and in Canada by Random House of Canada Ltd

      Library of Congress Cataloging-in-Publication Data
Teachings of Zen/compiled and translated by Thomas Cleary.
—1st ed.
          p.   cm.
    Includes bibliographical references.
    ISBN 1-57062-338-4 (pbk.: alk. paper)
    1. Zen Buddhism—Quotations, maxims, etc. I. Cleary,
Thomas F., 1949–   .
BQ9267.T43   1988
294.3'927—dc21   97-23349
                                          CIP

Contents

Introduction

Zen Buddhism emerged in China some fifteen centuries ago, to become one of the most dynamic spiritual movements of Asia for more than a thousand years.

After generations of experimentation with Buddhism, Zen masters found that enlightenment cannot be attained simply by literal adherence to dogma, or by mechanical performances of fixed systems of practices.

Returning to the source of Buddhism in personal experience of enlightenment, Zen teaching emphasized the liberation of subtle mental capacities from bondage to conditioned thinking habits and crude psychological propensities.

Conventional religious formats had externalized Buddhist teachings in the forms of myth, doctrine, and ritual. Zen masters internalized Buddhist teachings as allegories for perceptions, practices, and experiences of metaphysical principles, mental postures, psychological processes, psychic states, and spiritual capacities.

In projecting such interpretations of Buddhism, Zen teachers were not really innovating but concentrating on certain core teachings of the Buddhist scriptures.

Even the hallmark Zen teaching that "mind is Buddha" is not a Zen invention, but is found in scriptural sources.

Although they have been called iconoclastic, Zen masters did not oppose the practice of conventional religion, except where obsession with formalities of dogma and ritual inhibited spiritual experience of formless truth.

On a deeper level, Zen masters sought to restore and express the living meaning of religion and philosophy; the Zen teaching was to "study the living word, not the dead word." Not only did Zen reawaken Buddhism in this way, but it also revitalized Taoism, Confucianism, Shintoism, and shamanism, bringing out their higher spiritual dimensions.

The essentialist approach to Zen in practical presentation of the classical allegories and principles of Buddhism is illustrated with unparalleled clarity and simplicity by the great master Bankei (1622–1693), who had both Chinese and Japanese teachers but claimed to have rediscovered the spiritual reality of Zen through his own experience:

> When we look back on this life, we see that when people are born, no one has thoughts of joy, sadness, hatred, or bitterness. Are we not in the state of the buddha mind bequeathed by our parents? It is after birth that intelligence develops, and people learn bad

habits from others in the course of seeing and hearing them. As they grow up, their personal mental habits emerge, and they turn the buddha mind into a monster because of biased self-importance.

People are born with nothing but the unconceived buddha mind, but because of self-importance they want to get their own way, arguing and losing their temper yet claiming it is the stubbornness of others that makes them mad. Getting fixated on what others say, they turn the all-important unique buddha mind into a monster, mulling over useless things, repeating the same thoughts over and over again. They are so foolish they will not give up on things even if getting their own way would in any case prove to be futile. Folly is the cause of animality, so they are inwardly changing the all-important unique buddha mind into a paragon of animality.

Everyone is intelligent, but through lack of understanding they turn the buddha mind into all sorts of things—hungry ghost, monster, animal. Once you've become an animal, even if you hear truth you don't listen, or even if you do listen, being animal-like, you can't retain what you've heard.

Going from one hellish state to another, from one animalistic state to another, from one ghostly state to another, from darkness to darkness in an endless vicious cycle, you go on experiencing infinite misery for the bad things you have done, with never a break.

This can happen to anyone, once you've gone astray. Just understand the point of not turning the buddha mind into something else.

As soon as a single thought gets fixated on something, you become ordinary mortals. All delusion is like this. You pick up on something confronting you, turn the buddha mind into a monster because of your own self-importance, and go astray on account of your own ego.

Whatever it is confronting you, let it be. As long as you do not pick up on it and react with bias, just remaining in the buddha mind and not transforming it into something else, then delusion cannot occur. This is constant abiding in the unconceived buddha mind.

Everyone makes the mistake of supposing that acquired delusions produced by selfish desire and mental habits are inborn, and so they are unable to avoid confusion. . . .

As I listen to the people who come to me, all of them make the mistake of turning the buddha mind into thoughts, unable to stop, piling thoughts upon thoughts, resulting in the development of ingrained mental habits, which they then believe are inborn and unalterable.

Please understand; this is very important. Once you have unconsciously drifted into delusion, if your state of mind degenerates and you flow downward like a valley stream in a waterfall, there is no way back after you have fallen into vicious cycles.

Again, suppose that you have developed mental habits based on selfish desires. When people criticize things that suit your selfish mentality, you become angry and defensive — since they are, after all, bad things—and you rationalize them as good. When people praise things that do not suit your selfish mentality, you reject them—being, of course, good things —and you retort that they are bad.

Everything is like this. Delusion can make a defect seem like a virtue. Having fallen into ignorance, you go through all sorts of changes, degenerating further and further until you fall into hell, with precious little chance of regaining your humanity.

The most important thing is not to be self-centered; then you cannot fail to remain in the buddha mind spontaneously.

To want to be at least as good as others in everything is the worst thing there is. Wanting to be at least as good as others is called egotistic pride. As long as you don't wish to be superior to others, then you won't be inferior either.

Also, when people mistreat us, it is because we have pride. When we consider mistreatment from others to be due to our own defects and so we examine ourselves, then no one in the world is bad.

When angry thoughts arise, they turn the buddha

mind into a monster. But anger and delight both, being self-centered, obscure and confuse the luminous buddha mind, so that it goes around in vicious circles. Without subjective bias the buddha mind remains unconceived, so it does not revolve in circles. Let everyone understand this.

The following pages contain essential Zen teachings on realizing this original buddha mind in all of us. These teachings have been selected from the voluminous Zen canon for their accessibility, their clarity, and above all their practical effectiveness in fostering Zen concentrations and insights. This is Zen guidance presented by the masters for over a thousand years.

Teachings of Zen

The Mind Monarch

Observe the empty monarch of mind; mysterious, subtle, unfathomable, it has no shape or form, yet it has great spiritual power, able to extinguish a thousand troubles and perfect ten thousand virtues. Although its essence is empty, it can provide guidance. When you look at it, it has no form; call it, and it has a voice. It acts as a great spiritual leader; mental discipline transmits scripture.

Like salt in water, like adhesive in coloring, it is certainly there, but you don't see its form; so is the monarch of mind — dwelling inside the body, going in and out the senses, it responds freely to beings according to conditions, without hindrance, succeeding at all it does.

When you realize the fundamental, you perceive the mind; when you perceive the mind, you see Buddha. This mind is Buddha; the Buddha is mind. Keeping mindful of the buddha mind, the buddha mind is mindful of Buddha. If you want to realize early attainment, discipline your mind, regulate yourself. When you purify your habits and purify your mind, the mind itself is Buddha; there is no Buddha other than this mind monarch.

If you want to attain buddhahood, don't be stained by anything. Though the essence of mind is empty, the substance of greed and anger is solid. To enter this door to the source, sit straight and be Buddha. Once you've arrived at the other shore, you will attain the perfections.

People who seek the way, observe your own mind yourself. When you know the Buddha is within, and do not seek outside, then mind itself is Buddha, and Buddha is the mind. When the mind is clear, you perceive Buddha and understand the perceiving mind. Apart from mind is not Buddha; apart from Buddha is not mind. If not for Buddha, nothing is fathomed; there is no competence at all.

If you cling to emptiness and linger in quiescence, you will bob and sink herein: the buddhas and bodhisattvas do not rest their minds this way. Great people who clarify the mind understand this mystic message; body and mind naturally sublimated, their action is unchanging. Therefore the wise release the mind to be independent and free.

Do not say the mind monarch is empty in having no essential nature; it can cause the physical body to do wrong or do right. Neither being nor nonbeing, it is concealed and revealed without fixation. Although the essence of mind is empty, it can be ordinary and can be saintly: therefore I urge you to guard it yourself carefully — a moment of contrivance, and you go back to bobbing and sinking.

The knowledge of the pure clean mind is as yellow gold to the world; the spiritual treasury of wisdom is all in the body and mind. The uncreated spiritual treasure is neither shallow nor deep. The buddhas and bodhisattvas understand this basic mind; for those who have the chance to encounter it, it is not past, future, or present.

Fu Shan-hui (487–569)

Five Types of Meditation Method

Know the essence of mind. Its intrinsic essence is pure clarity. It is essentially the same as a buddha.

Know the functions of the mind. Its functions produce the treasury of teachings. When its activity is always silent, myriad illusions become suchness.

Constantly be aware, without stopping. When the aware mind is present, it senses the formlessness of things.

Constantly see your body as empty and quiet, inside and outside communing in sameness. Plunge the body into the realm of reality, where there has never been any obstruction.

Keep to unity without shifting. With constant presence, whether active or still, the student can see the buddha nature clearly.

Tao-hsin (580–651)

Let Your Mind Be Free

It has been asked, "How should those who enter the path apply their minds?"

All things are originally uncreated and presently undying. Just let your mind be free; you don't have to restrain it.

See directly and hear directly; come directly and go directly. When you must go, then go; when you must stay, then stay.

This is the true path. A scripture says, "Conditional existence is the site of enlightenment, insofar as you know it as it really is."

Niu-t'ou Hui-chung (683–769)

No Performance

It has been asked, "If one wants to practice the path now, what technique should one perform to attain liberation?"

People who see buddhahood immediately realize the mind source without performing techniques. When you clearly see buddha nature, this very mind is Buddha, because it is neither illusory nor real. A scripture says, "Directly abandoning expedients, just expound the unsurpassed way."

Hui-chung

The Normal Mind Is the Way

The way does not require cultivation; just don't defile it. What is defilement? As long as you have a fluctuating mind, artificiality, or compulsive tendencies, all of this is defilement.

If you want to understand the way directly, the normal mind is the way. What I call the normal mind is free from artificiality: in it there is no right or wrong, no grasping or rejection, no extinction or permanence, no banality or sanctity. A scripture says, "Neither the conduct of ordinary people nor the conduct of saints, it is the conduct of enlightening beings."

Right now, as you walk, stand, sit, and recline, responding to situations and dealing with people, all is the way. The way is the realm of reality. No matter how many the countless inconceivable functions, they are not beyond the realm of reality. If it were not so, how could we speak of the teaching of the ground of mind, how could we speak of the inexhaustible lamp?

All phenomena are mental phenomena; all names are named by mind. All phenomena arise from mind; mind is the root of all phenomena. A scripture says, "When you know the mind and arrive at the root source, in that sense you may be said to be a devotee."

The equivalency of terms, the equivalency of meanings, and the equivalency of all truths are wholly one, without adulteration. If you can attain situational free mastery of the teachings, when you define the realm of reality, all is the realm of reality; when you define true suchness, all is true suchness. If you speak in terms of abstract designs, all realities are abstract designs; if you speak in terms of concrete facts, all realities are concrete facts. Bring up one, and a thousand follow; abstract principle and concrete fact are no different. All are inconceivable functions; there is no other principle. All derive from the operation of mind.

Metaphorically, it is like the fact that there is a plurality of reflections of the moon but no plurality in the real moon. There is a plurality of water sources but not a plurality in the essence of water. There is plurality in myriad forms, but there is no plurality in space. There is plurality in principles expounded but no plurality in uninhibited intelligence.

All kinds of establishments derive from one mind: you may set them up, and you may dismantle them; both are inconceivable functions, and inconceivable functions are all your own. If there is no place to stand apart from reality, then where you stand is real; all is the structure of your own house. If anyone is otherwise, then who is it?

All things are Buddhist teachings; all things are liberating. Liberation is true suchness, and nothing is apart from true suchness. Walking, standing, sitting, and reclining are all inconceivable acts.

This does not depend on the time: scripture says,

"Everywhere, everyplace, is Buddha considered to be." A buddha is one who is capable of humanity, who has knowledge and wisdom, who accurately perceives potentials and states of mind and can cut through the web of doubts of all living beings, getting out of entanglements such as being and nonbeing, so that both profane and sacred feelings end, and personality and phenomena are both empty: then a buddha turns the incomparable wheel of teaching that transcends calculation and measurement, unobstructed in action, communicating both concrete facts and abstract principles.

It is like clouds rising in the sky: suddenly there, then gone without a trace. And it is like drawing a pattern on water: it neither is born nor passes away. This is cosmic peace and eternal rest. When it is enclosed, it is called the matrix of the realization of suchness; when it emerges from enclosure, it is called the cosmic body of reality.

The body of reality is infinite; its substance neither increases nor decreases. It can be great or small, square or round; it manifests visible forms in accordance with things and beings, like the moon reflected in water. Its effusive function does not plant roots: it does not exhaust deliberate action and does not dwell in nondoing. Deliberate action is a function of nonartificiality; nonartificiality is the basis of deliberate action. Because of not being fixated on the basis, one is said to be independent, like space.

As for the meanings of birth and death of mind and

true suchness of mind, the true suchness of mind is like a clear mirror reflecting images: the mind is like the mirror, the images are like phenomena. If the mind grasps phenomena, then it gets involved in external causes and conditions; this is the meaning of the birth and death of mind. If it does not grasp phenomena, this is the meaning of true suchness of mind.

Followers hear about seeing buddha nature; enlightening beings see buddha nature with their eyes. When you realize nonduality, terms are equivalent, having no difference in essence but not being the same in usage. What is called consciousness in a state of delusion is called knowledge in the enlightened state; following principle is called enlightenment, following things is called delusion.

When you are deluded, that means you have lost sight of your own original mind. When you are enlightened, that means you have realized your own original mind. Once enlightened you are forever enlightened and do not become deluded anymore. It is like when the sunlight comes out, it does not combine with darkness; when the sunlight of knowledge and wisdom emerge, they are not together with the darkness of afflictions.

When you understand mind and objects, then idle imaginings do not arise. When idle imaginings do not arise, this is acceptance of the uncreated. What is fundamentally there is there now; you don't need to cultivate the path and sit meditating. Not cultivating and not sitting is the pure meditation of those who realize suchness.

Now, if you see this principle truly and accurately and do not fabricate any actions but pass your life according to your lot, fulfilling your minimal needs wherever you are, disciplined conduct increasingly taking effect, accumulating pure actions — as long as you can be like this, why worry about not attaining mastery?

Ma-tsu (709–788)

The Body of Reality

The essence of mind is formless; this itself is the subtle body of reality. The essence of mind is inherently empty; this itself is the infinite body of space. Demonstrating arrays of practices is the body of reality of virtues. The body of reality is the root of myriad emanations, which are named according to the situation. Its knowledge and function are endless; this is the inexhaustible treasury.

Ta-chu (eighth century)

Get the Root

You should each individually clarify your own mind, getting to the root without pursuing the branches. Just get the root, and the branches come of themselves. If you want to get the root, just get to know your mind. This mind is basically the root of all mundane and supramundane phenomena. As long as the mind does not become obsessed with all good and bad, you will realize that all things are basically just so.

Ta-mei (ca. 805)

Verbal Teachings

All verbal teachings are just to cure diseases. Because diseases are not the same, the remedies are also different. That is why it is sometimes said that there is Buddha, and sometimes it is said that there is no Buddha.

True words are those that actually cure sickness; if the cure manages to heal, then all are true words. If they can't effectively cure sickness, all are false words.

True words are false words when they give rise to views. False words are true words when they cut off the delusions of sentient beings. Because disease is unreal, there is only unreal medicine to cure it.

Pai-chang (720–814)

Inward and Outward Views

To cling to oneself as Buddha, oneself as Zen or the way, making that an understanding, is called clinging to the inward view. Attainment by causes and conditions, practice and realization, is called the outward view. Master Pao-chih said, "The inward view and the outward view are both mistaken."

Pai-chang

Seeking

A buddha is one who does not seek. In seeking this, you turn away from it. The principle is the principle of nonseeking; when you seek it, you lose it.

If you cling to nonseeking, this is the same as seeking. If you cling to nonstriving, this is the same as striving.

Thus the *Diamond Cutter Scripture* says, "Do not grasp truth, do not grasp untruth, and do not grasp that which is not untrue."

It also says, "The truth that the buddhas find has no reality or unreality."

Pai-chang

Liberation in All Places

Don't seek a buddha, don't seek a teaching, don't seek a community. Don't seek virtue, knowledge, intellectual understanding, and so on. When feelings of defilement and purity are ended, still don't hold to this nonseeking and consider it right. Don't dwell at the point of ending, and don't long for heavens or fear hells. When you are unhindered by bondage or freedom, then this is called liberation of mind and body in all places.

Pai-chang

A Method of Awakening

First set aside all involvements and concerns; do not remember or recollect anything at all, whether good or bad, mundane or transcendental. Do not engage in thoughts. Let go of body and mind, setting them free.

When the mind is like wood or stone, you do not explain anything, and the mind does not go anywhere, then the mind ground becomes like space, wherein the sun of wisdom naturally appears. It is as though the clouds had opened and the sun emerged.

Just put an end to all fettering connections, and feelings of greed, hatred, craving, defilement and purity, all come to an end. Unmoved in the face of inner desires and external influences, not choked up by perception and cognition, not confused by anything, naturally endowed with all virtues and the inconceivable use of spiritual capacities, this is someone who is free.

Having a mind neither stilled nor disturbed in the presence of all things in the environment, neither concentrated nor distracted, passing through all sound and form without lingering or obstruction, is called being a wayfarer.

Not setting in motion good or evil, right or wrong, not clinging to a single thing, not rejecting a single thing, is called being a member of the great caravan.

Not being bound by any good or evil, emptiness or existence, defilement or purity, striving or nonstriving, mundanity or transcendence, virtue or knowledge, is called enlightened wisdom.

Once affirmation and negation, like and dislike, approval and disapproval, and all various opinions and feelings come to an end and cannot bind you, then you are free wherever you may be. This is what is called a bodhisattva at the moment of inspiration immediately ascending to the stage of buddhahood.

Pai-chang

This Abundant Light

You guard a spiritual thing: it isn't something you could make, and it isn't something you can describe. In this ground of ours, there is no Buddha, no nirvana, and no path to practice, no doctrine to actualize. The way is not within existence or nonexistence — what method would one then practice? This abundant light, wherever you are, in every situation, is itself the great way.

Tan-hsia (739–824)

Mystic Understanding

Mystic understanding of truth is not perception or cognition. That is why it is said that you arrive at the original source by stopping the mind, so it is called the enlightened state of being as is, the ultimately independent free individual.

Nan-ch'uan (748–834)

Absolute Truth

The body of truth is not constructed; it does not fall into any category. Truth is unshakable; it does not depend on the objects of the six senses. Therefore scripture says buddha nature is constant, while mind is inconstant. That is the sense in which knowledge is not the way and mind is not Buddha.

For now, do not say mind is Buddha; do not understand in terms of perception and cognition. This thing originally does not have all those names.

Nan-ch'uan

Practice

Someone asked Nan-ch'uan, "How does one cultivate practice?"

Nan-ch'uan replied, "It cannot be thought up. To tell people to cultivate in such and such a way, or to practice in such and such a way, is very difficult."

The questioner now asked, "Then will you let students cultivate practice at all?"

Nan-ch'uan answered, "I cannot stop you."

"How should I practice?"

Nan-ch'uan said, "Do what you have to do; don't just follow behind others."

Formless Mind

The formless mind can operate brilliance, responding to sound, responding to form, illuminating wherever it is directed. Even though it may be localized, it is not local; while going along with the flow high and low, it is altogether inconceivable. If you look for it, it has no head; and it has no tail: where do its surges of radiant light come from? Just this right now is all mental: the mind is used to clarify mind, and mind reverts to spontaneity. Since it does not abide anywhere, where can you look for it? Its operation has no tracks and no traces. Get to know the person who is clearly seeking right now — don't disregard this and seek another aim.

Kao-ch'eng (n.d.)

Spirituality

If there were any object, any doctrine, that could be given to you to hold on to or understand, it would reduce you to bewilderment and externalism. It's just a spiritual openness, with nothing that can be grasped; it is pure everywhere, its light clearly penetrating, outwardly and inwardly luminous through and through.

Te-shan (d. 867)

Liberation

Don't love sagehood; sagehood is an empty name. There is no special truth but this radiant spiritual openness, unobstructed and free. It is not attained by adornment and cultivated realization. From the buddhas to the Zen masters, all have transmitted this teaching, by which they attained liberation.

Te-shan

The Business of Zen

One day the governor of the province asked Mu-chou (780–877), "What is the business of Zen?"

Mu-chou said, "Come here, come here."

The governor approached; Mu-chou said, "You sure can talk nonsense!"

The governor was speechless. Finally Mu-chou asked, "Whom have you seen?"

The governor said that he had seen such-and-such an old adept. Mu-chou asked, "What else?" The governor replied that he had read scriptures. Mu-chou suddenly hit his chair and said, "In the teachings, what is this called?"

The governor said, "It is not spoken of in the teachings."

Mu-chou said, "In the teachings it says, 'Productive labor as a means of livelihood is not contrary to the truth.' What about that?"

The governor had no reply.

Evaluating Teachers

When I was journeying, I didn't choose communities on the basis of whether or not they had material provisions; I was only concerned with seeing whether their perception indicated some capacity. If so, then I might stay for a summer or a winter; but if they were low-minded, I'd leave in two or three days. Although I called on more than sixty prominent teachers, barely one or two had great perception. The rest hardly had real true knowledge — they just want your donations.

Ta-sui (834–919)

The Essential Nature

The essential nature is originally pure and endowed with myriad virtues, but there come to be differentiations because of following conditions that are tainted or pure. Therefore sages realize this and only use it in pure ways, thus attaining enlightenment, while ordinary people miss it and only use it in tainted ways, sinking into moribund routines. Their essence is not two; that is why the scriptures on transcendent wisdom say that "there is no duality, no division, because there is no disjunction, no separateness."

Ta-sui

A Priceless Jewel

Each of you has a priceless jewel in your own body. It radiates light through your eyes, shining through the mountains, rivers, and earth. It radiates light through your ears, taking in all sounds, good and bad. It radiates light through your six senses day and night. This is also called absorption in light. You yourself do not recognize it, but it is in your physical body, supporting it inside and out, not letting it tip over. Even if you are carrying a double load of rocks over a single-log bridge, it still doesn't let you fall over. What is this? If you seek in the slightest, then it cannot be seen.

Ta-an (d. 883)

Free-Flowing

All things are free-flowing, untrammeled — what bondage is there, what entanglement? You create your own difficulty and ease therein. The mind source pervades the ten directions with one continuity; those of the most excellent faculties understand naturally.

Tzu-hu (800–880)

Independence

There is no other task but to know your own original face. This is called independence; the spirit is clear and free. If you say there is some particular doctrine or patriarchy, you'll be totally cheated. Just look into your heart; there is a transcendental clarity. Just have no greed and no dependency and you will immediately attain certainty.

Yen-t'ou (828–887)

Degeneration of Zen

Ninety years ago, I saw more than eighty teachers from the school of the great master Ma-tsu. Each of them was an adept, unlike the teachers today who produce branches and tendrils upon branches and tendrils. The generality of them are far from sagehood, and each generation is worse than the last.

How about Nan-ch'uan's usual saying that we should act in the midst of different kinds? How do you understand this? Nowadays yellow-mouthed punks give complicated talks at crossroads in exchange for food to eat, seeking obeisance, gathering crowds of three to five hundred, saying, "I am the teacher, you are the students."

Chao-chou (778–897)

The Normal Mind

Chao-chou was asked, "Is a person with a normal mind still to be taught?"

Chao-chou said, "I don't go through such a person's door."

The questioner asked, "Then wouldn't it be someone sunk into the beyond?"

Chao-chou retorted, "A fine 'normal mind'!"

No Fooling

You come here looking for sayings and talks, novel expressions and elegant lines, uselessly taking to verbalization. I am old and my energy is not up to par; I'm a dull speaker and have no idle talk for you. If you ask me questions, I answer in accord with your questions, but I have no mysterious marvel that can be conveyed to you, and I won't have you get fixated.

I never assert the existence of Buddha and Dharma, of ordinary person and sage, either in the beyond or the here and now; and I have no intention of sitting here tying you people down. You go through a thousand changes, but all of it is you people conceiving interpretations, carrying them with you, experiencing the results of your own doings. I have nothing here for you, and nothing exoteric or esoteric to explain to you, no appearance or intention to represent to you.

T'ou-tzu (819–914)

Natural

To speak of practicing the path is an expression of encouragement, a term of inducement; there has never been any doctrine to give people, just transmission of various expedient techniques. These are for expressing the essential idea, to get people to know their own minds. Ultimately there is no doctrine to get, no path to practice. Therefore it is said, "The path of enlightenment is natural."

Lung-ya (834–920)

The Ocean of Knowledge

Have you gotten familiar with the ocean of intuitive knowledge of the essence and forms of pure original suchness? If you have not gotten familiar with it, how about the green mountains here before your eyes — do you see them?

If you say you see them, how do you see? If you say you don't see, how can the green mountains be called invisible?

Do you understand? It is simply that your ocean of intuitive knowledge of the essence and forms of pure original suchness is equipped with seeing and hearing.

If you understand, it is simply as such; if you don't understand, it is still simply as such.

Hsuan-sha (ninth to tenth century)

Your Own Experience

Every reality is eternal, every essence is as is: just don't seek outwardly. If you have a great root of faith, the buddhas are just states of your own experience; whether you are walking, standing, sitting, or lying down, never is it not this.

My speaking directly to you now is already pressing the free into servitude. Would you agree to speak thus? And how do you understand agreeing or not agreeing?

Hsuan-sha

No Thing

There is no thing to Buddhism — it can enliven people, and it can kill people too. Seeing essential nature and becoming enlightened penetrates all time.

Hsuan-sha

The Reality of Mind

The earth and the sky are entirely composed of mind, but how do you explain the principle of being composed of mind? And how do you explain the reality of mind without form pervading the ten directions? There is no part that does not come from compassion producing knowledge, there is no part that does not come from knowledge activating compassion, and there is no part that does not come from compassion and knowledge equally illumining the ocean of essential nature, pervading the universe, completely fluid and free.

Knowing the light and the dark, matter and emptiness, compassion and knowledge equally wind up at the door of concentration of kindness, with reward, response, and reality, independent and free, widely benefiting the world. The whole earth and open space are both manifestations of the door of concentration of kindness. That is why it is said that the reality of mind without form pervades the ten directions.

Hsuan-sha

Wide Open

The way of buddhas is wide open, without any stages. The door of nothing is the door to liberation; having no intention is the will to help others. It is not within past, present, and future, so it cannot rise and sink; setups are counter to reality, because it is not in the realm of the created.

Move, and you produce the root of birth and death; be still, and you get drunk in the village of oblivion. If movement and stillness are both erased, you fall into empty annihilation; if movement and stillness are both withdrawn, you presume upon buddha nature.

You must be like a dead tree or cold ashes in the face of objects and situations while acting responsively according to the time, without losing proper balance. A mirror reflects a multitude of images without their confusing its brilliance; birds fly through the sky without mixing up the color of the sky.

Hsuan-sha

The Great Task

As long as you have not accomplished the great task and are not in communion with the bloodline of the source, you must avoid memorizing sayings and living inside conceptual consciousness. Has it not been said, "Concepts act as robbers, consciousness becomes waves"? Everyone has been swept away and drowned. There is no freedom in that.

If you have not mastered the great task, nothing compares to stopping, in the sense of quiet cessation, the purifying and quieting of the body and mind. At all times avoid dwelling obsessively on things, and it will be easy to unveil *this*.

Ku-shan (d. ca. 940)

The Object of Investigation

Ku-shan was asked, "What is the basic object of investigation?"

He replied, "How one has gotten to such a state."

Names and Actualities

An ancient said, "'Buddha' and 'Dharma' are constructed teaching methods; the terms *Zen* and *Tao* are talk for pacifying children." The names have no relation to actualities, actualities have no relation to names; if you cling to names, you will be blocked from the mystery.

That is why I have told you that sayings do not correspond to potential, words do not set forth actualities. Those who accept words perish; those who linger over sayings get lost. When you have caught the fish, you forget the trap; when you have gotten the meaning, you forget the words. We use a net to catch fish; the fish are not the net.

Ku-shan

What Is Disturbing You

What is disturbing you and making you uneasy is that there are things outside and mind inside. Therefore even when the ordinary and the holy are one reality, there still remains a barrier of view. So it is said that as long as views remain you are ordinary; when feelings are forgotten you're a buddha. I advise you, don't seek reality, just stop views.

Fa-yen (885–958)

The Eye of the Heart

To expound the vehicle to the source and bring out the great teaching, it is necessary to attain thorough clarity of the objective eye; only then can you perceive the distinction between the initiate and the naive. Because reality and falsehood have the same source, it's hard to tell them apart, like water and milk in the same vessel. I always use the eye in my heart to observe external appearances. I keep observing until I discern the true from the false. How could anyone who doesn't do this be called a teacher?

Tung-shan Shou-ch'u (ca. 910/15–990/95)

The Normal Mind

Tung-shan was asked, "The normal mind is the way; what is the normal mind?"

He replied, "Not picking things up along the road."

Excess

If you want to seek too much, it may hinder the way. For your part, can you say your work is done? If not, then a thousand kinds of clever talk do not enhance your mind; what is the reason for ten thousand kinds of thought?

Chih-men (fl. ca. 1000–1020)

The Pivotal Point

"When you try to set your mind on it, you miss it; when you stir your thoughts, you turn away from it. If you do not try and do not stir, you are making your living in stagnant water. What is the pivotal point for a Zennist?" Is there any benefit in this ancient saying? If you say there is benefit, it binds you fatally with words. If you say there is no benefit, what is the intention?

This is why it is said, "The heart of nirvana is easy to realize; knowledge of differentiation is hard to clarify."

Chih-men

What Thing

What thing is not attained when painstakingly
sought?

What thing comes of itself without being sought?

What thing does not break under the blow of an
iron hammer?

What thing closes by night and opens by day?

Chih-men

Truth and Words

There is originally no word for truth, but the way to it is revealed by words. The way originally has no explanation, but reality is made clear by explanation. That is why the buddhas appeared in the world with many expedient methods; the whole canon dispenses medicines according to diseases.

Shih-shuang (986–1039)

The Cause of Misery

Greed is the basic cause of misery; if you extinguish greed, then it has no basis. If you have no greed, you are clean and free wherever you are; the mountains, rivers, and earth do not block the light of your eyes.

She-hsien (tenth to eleventh century)

Eyes for Study

Zen study can only be done with the eyes for Zen study; if you are simply attracted to others' sayings and memorize them, you will not be able to cut through yourself.

Shen-ting (tenth to eleventh century)

No Sectarian Style

I have no sayings or statements to have you understand, and no sayings or statements to have you study. And I have no sectarian style to have you set up. I just distinguish right and wrong for you, so that you will not jump to conclusions and think you have attained when you have not.

Ch'eng-ku (fl. ca. 1037)

Look into Yourself

Space has no inside or outside; the same is so of the reality of mind. If you comprehend space, this is arriving at the principle of reality as such.

This was the way of the ancient masters, but later descendants couldn't continue it. That is because it is easy to understand but hard to see.

To understand as soon as it's brought up is called conceiving interpretation according to words; it's also called dependent penetration. It is also called parrot understanding. It is not personal realization and personal awakening. Therefore feelings of doubt do not stop.

Because they have no basis to rely on, and their habit-ridden consciousness is manic, people produce idiosyncratic views. They say, "I won't enter this deep pit of liberation," and "What end is there to running around in this spiritual realm? Why not seek a way out?" Or they say, "I have something transcendental within me," or "I have the road to penetrating liberation within me." When asked what the road to penetrating liberation is, some say, "Donkeys pick wet spots to piss," or "In spring the grass is deep green." Taking up the way of the ancient masters, instead they uphold verbal teachings as the ultimate model.

This is called slighting mind and esteeming doctrine,

abandoning the root and pursuing the branches, like a dog chasing a clod. For a hundred and ten years now, everyone's been like this. Master Hsueh-feng said, "The grand masters have passed away, buried in the weeds by you people today."

If you manage to enter in by the way of the ancient masters, that will be like a hundred thousand suns and moons, liberating all sentient beings in the universe. If you enter into verbal teachings, that will be like the light of a firefly, and you won't even be able to save yourself. Why? Because it is still sterile wisdom. Detach from literal knowledge and look into yourself.

Ch'eng-ku

Whoring for Appearances

If you don't know there is an original self, and do not know there is such a thing as the road beyond, and instead learn to question and answer based on writings and words, what relevance is there? With three or five notebooks of extracts and notes, wherever you go to spend the summer or winter in the congregation of a master, you ask for more instruction on every item, right from the start, and talk about ascent and descent, perception and function, vertical and horizontal, becoming a clear Zennist, not relying on a single thing. You say the issue of your own self is clear, and keep it in your chest as the ultimate rule. Eventually you want to be called a Zen master and to open eyes for later people. How much you bury away the ancient masters and misguide later people! If you try to counter birth and death with things like this, will it work? Even if you immediately have a great insight and a great awakening, and can talk like clouds and rain, all you have gained is a slippery tongue — you are further and further from the way. That's what is called being a whore for appearances.

Ch'eng-ku

Cease and Desist

It is essential for you to cease and desist from your previously held knowledge, opinions, interpretations, and understandings. It is not accomplished by stopping the mind; temporary relinquishment is not the way — it fools you into wasting body and mind, without accomplishing anything at all in the end.

I suggest to you that nothing compares to ceasing and desisting. There is nowhere for you to apply your mind. Just be like an imbecile twenty-four hours a day. You have to be spontaneous and buoyant, your mind like space, yet without any measurement of space. You have to be beyond light and dark, no Buddhism, body, or mind, year in and year out. If anything is not forgotten, you've spent your life in vain. That is why it is said, "Even if you learn things pertaining to buddhahood, that too is misuse of mind. You have to be free of preoccupations; you have to be normal."

Nevertheless, even so, it is undeniably hard to find people. Not just now — it has always been hard to find people. It was hard even in ancient times; how much the more so nowadays when people who study things are all drawn into weeds by ignorant old baldies! That is why it is said, "Our eyes were originally right, but went wrong because of teachers."

Ch'eng-ku

58

Facing Suchness

Fog locks the endless sky, wind rises over the vast plains; all plants and trees roar the great lion's roar, expounding universal wisdom; the buddhas of past, present, and future are at your feet, turning the wheel of the great teaching.

If you can understand, you will not expend effort at random. If you do not understand, don't say this mountain is steep — the highest peak is still ahead.

Yang-ch'i (992–1049)

The Primordial

"There is something before heaven and earth, form-less and basically silent; the master of all forms, it does not fade along with the seasons." Tell me, what is this? Do you know? If you know, the whole universe and everything in it is luminously clear. If you don't know, when confronted by things you cannot turn around.

Tao-wu Wu-chen (fl. ca. 1025–1060)

Where Will You Seek?

What is there to Buddhism? Old masters have said, "There is no matter, so be unconcerned," and "The body of truth is uncreated and is not subsumed by any categories." An ancient worthy said, "When you don't believe in Buddha or bodhi, understanding of emptiness is foremost." That is why it is said, "Speaking of buddhas and Zen masters, talking about mysteries and marvels, is all saying too much or too little."

This being so, then where will you seek? You must have the eye to journey before you can.

Fa-hua (fl. ca 1000–1056)

Straight and True

Sit straight, and before you buy shoes measure your feet. Looking around this way and that isn't worth a cent.

Ta-yü Shou-chih (d. ca. 1060)

Waking Up

When you know illusion, you become unattached, without exercising any technique. When you detach from illusion, you wake up, without going through any process. Shakyamuni Buddha opened up a thousand gates and ten thousand doors all at once; someone who is spiritually sharp will immediately act on that. As for those who shilly-shally, you and I are going in different directions.

Tsu-hsin (eleventh century)

Heart of Hearts

This very mind, heart of hearts, is Buddha, the most spiritual being in the universe. Wondrous functions free in all ways may be charming, but the whole lot of it is not as good as authentic truth of mind.

Do not have the arrogance to pretend you are seeking enlightenment; enlightenment cannot be seen. Do not have the arrogance to pretend you are getting rid of afflictions; afflictions have no front or back. Before the appearance of signs, there is fundamentally no change. If you speak of understanding or nonunderstanding, it is all three necks and two heads. If you go on asking "How?" and "Huh?" — what a pain, this Buddha!

Tsu-hsin

Eyes and Feet

If you only understand your self and not the environment, you have eyes but no feet. If you understand the environment but not your self, you have feet but no eyes. In either case there is something on your chest all the time. Since there is something on your chest, uneasiness is always present, and you get stuck along the way. How can you attain peace? A spiritual ancestor said, "If you cling to it, you lose measure and inevitably fall into a false path. Let it go and be natural; essence neither goes nor stays."

Tsu-hsin

Testing Seekers

I have tested all the Zen seekers in the world with four pivotal sayings:

"There is life within death."

"There is death within life."

"There is permanent death in death."

"There is permanent life in life."

Now tell me, what do all the Zen seekers in the world use to test me?

Ssu-hsin (eleventh century)

Human Sentiment

Buddhism does not obey human sentiments. The elders everywhere all open their mouths wide, saying "I understand Zen, I understand Tao!" But tell me, do they understand or not?

As for those who sit in cesspits for no reason, deceiving spirits and fooling ghosts, even if you killed a thousand or ten thousand of them and fed them to the dogs, what would be wrong with that?

There's also a type of Zen followers who get bewitched by those foxes with their eyes wide open, quite unaware of it themselves. Plunging into pouring piss, they don't even feel disgusted.

Hey! You are all adults! How can you accept this? What should you do yourself?

Chen-ching (exiled 1080)

Individual Realization

This thing cannot be learned, cannot be taught, cannot be transmitted: it can only be attained by individual realization. Once you've attained realization, you are content, unpreoccupied, thoroughly lucid, clear and at ease. All spiritual capacities and miracle working are inherent endowments and need not be sought elsewhere.

Chen-ching

Preparedness

It's hard to find people ready for Buddhism. Some do not believe in the fact of the Buddha within themselves, only relying on a little bit of the influence of the ancients, on imitation wisdom. The domain of their knowledge is doctrines on characteristics of meditation; in action, they turn away from enlightenment and get mixed up in the dust, stuck and unable to get free. If students come to them, it is like an imprint stamping clay; they successively hand on the imprint, not only fooling themselves but also fooling others.

I have no Buddhism to give anyone. I just have a sword — whoever comes, I cut down, so their lives cannot go on and their seeing and hearing disappear: then I meet them before their parents gave birth to them. If I see them go forward, I cut them off.

However, though the sword is sharp, it does not cut the innocent. Is there anyone who is innocent?

Chen-ching

The Pure Luminous Body

Shakyamuni Buddha said that the continuing birth and death of all beings is because they don't know the pure luminous body of the eternal true essence of mind, and employ all sorts of false thoughts; because these thoughts are not real, there is habitual repetition.

Do you want birth and death not to continue, the falsely thinking mind to die out? Just directly get to know the pure luminous body of the eternal true essence of mind in yourself. Then birth and death naturally will not continue, and everyone will rejoice together. This is what is called attainment once and for all time.

If you cannot believe in it and won't listen, then you remain sunk in habit-ridden consciousness, an ocean of ignorance.

Chen-ching

Removing Bonds

I do not understand Zen, I do not understand Tao: I only know how to dissolve glue and remove bonds, to give medicines according to ailments.

There is no Zen to study, no Tao to learn. Abandoning the fundamental to pursue trivia, busily working on externals, is not as good as coming back to get to know your own citadel.

In the citadel is your own spiritual monarch to honor, who answers a hundredfold when called once, who wants all people to wake up themselves.

Come, come! What you must do is put down your previous knowledge and views of Buddhism all at once; then the mental stamp of your own cosmic Buddha will be clear through and through.

Chen-ching

Only Mind

Before you have realized objects are only mind, you produce all sorts of discriminations; after you have realized objects are only mind, discrimination does not arise. When you know all things are only mind, then you let go of the forms of external objects. But what about the earth, the mountains and rivers, light and dark, matter and space: with all things right before you, what principle of letting go can you speak of?

Even if you understand this, you are still just halfway. You must realize there is yet another opening going beyond.

Yun-feng Wen-yueh (d. ca. 1060)

Truth and the Way

The way is the perennial Way, the truth is the perennial Truth: don't misapply body and mind chasing after sayings. This is why it is said that "even the slightest object is dust; as soon as you arouse intent, you're confused by hallucination."

Yun-feng

Stop

If you can stop right now, then stop; if you seek a time of completion, there is no time of completion. If you make up intellectual understanding of this matter based on words, or try to figure it out conceptually, you are as far from it as the sky is from earth.

For people of great power, cutting in two with one slash is not yet attainment; how much less is being called away by someone else to give muddled explanations in an abbot's room, citing scripture and treatise, bringing up senses and objects, material phenomena, transcendence and immanence, being and nonbeing, gain and loss! Some day you will die without having found your place.

Yun-feng

Warped Understanding

In recent times there is another kind of Zen master who enjoys fame for twenty or thirty years just telling people not to pay attention to the sayings of others, calling this "passing through sound and form." When they are asked about the east, they answer about the west, considering that "expression beyond convention." Passing on this warped understanding, they have thus confused and damaged Zen teaching, fooling and deluding younger generations.

Yun-feng

Absolute and Relative

When the absolute is absolute, it is incomplete; within completeness there is also the relative. When the relative is relative, it is not material; even within matter, completeness remains. Deep in the night, there's the energy that brings on dawn; when the sun is at its peak, it lights up the skies.

I-ch'ing (1032–1083)

Concepts and Emotions

Zen is not in conceptual understanding; how can the way be sought by emotions?

I-ch'ing

Original Zen

In the original Zen school, an authentic meeting was not a matter of climbing up into a high pulpit and setting out verbal points. Why? This is why it is said that if verbal points miss, home's ten thousand miles away.

You simply have to let go over a cliff, willingly accept the experience, and revive after annihilation. It will be impossible to deceive you.

This is why past sages skillfully employed expedient techniques, eventually setting out many methods, setting them up on a nonabiding basis. Since the basis is nonabiding, it can respond to a multitude of conditions, just like an enormous bell sounding when struck, like the moonlight reflecting in a thousand rivers. This is unconditional compassion responding sensitively according to potential, a nondual message divided according to faculties and natures. Although the teachings take many tracks, the ideal goal is one.

Hui-lin (1020–1099)

The Path

Truth has no this or that, the path has no ordinary or holy: throughout the ages it has been smooth, beyond all cultivation and realization. Those who get it produce lotuses in scarlet flames, those who lose it grasp at reflections in aquamarine pools.

The reason you have not attained it yet is generally because of the present time. I will sweep away thoughts of both good and bad all at once for you, and even get you not to make extinction your home, not to make emptiness your seat, and not to make myriad practices your clothing, so in action you are like the flight of a bird, and in stillness you are like open space.

Fu-jung (1042–1118)

A Shortcut

A shortcut into the path is to be inwardly empty and outwardly quiet, like water that is clear and still, myriad images reflecting in it, neither sinking nor floating, all things spontaneously so.

Fu-jung

Avoiding Residual Trouble

"All realities are uncreated, all realities are imperishable" — if you can understand thus, the buddhas are always present. You should take the mind that frantically seeks every day and use it to investigate this matter. After a long, long time it will naturally become clear. If you do not do this, you are living and dying in vain. An ancient said, "Make an effort; you must understand in this life. Don't subject yourself to residual trouble over the ages."

Huai-shan (fl. ca. 1115)

Six Roads

There are six roads before you: one is suitable for travel, five are not.

First, don't rub your eyes and create optical illusions on the subtle ground of the sages.

Second, don't take servant for master on the ground of ordinary reality.

Third, don't play with physical energy in a state of light.

Fourth, don't be an escapist in the room of nothing.

Fifth, don't talk of yellow and red in a nest of complications.

The sixth road is the only one I'd let you go on. But tell me, how do you travel this road?

Understand?

If not for your footgear's wearing out, how do you notice the forked road is long?

Huai-shan

Self-Defeat

The ultimate way is without difficulty; those who seek it make their own hardship. The true mind is originally pure; those who exercise it make their own defilement.

Hui-k'ung (1096–1158)

The Living Eye

The living eye of Zen sees clearly through the heavens: the livelihood of the six senses takes place everywhere, without borrowing the form or appearance of another.

Tzu-te (1090–1159)

Looking for and Looking At

I have something here: when you look at it, it's there,
but when you look for it, it's not. What is it?

Tzu-te

The Black Pearl

When you are completely clear, there is no subjective distortion; when you are completely pure, there is true perception. But even if you are thus through and through, this is still not the transcendental key. When the wind and waves have died out, the ocean of mind is as is; when you get to the bottom of the ocean of mind, for the first time you see the black pearl.

Tzu-te

Fabrications

As I see people pursuing the path today, none of them seem to be in accord with it. Why is this so? Some of them control their minds to make them settled within, others gather in their thoughts to induce stabilization. All of them are fabrications. In reality, this is not inner mastery at all.

If they are able to want to see, these people have to turn around this mindless state; would they have no understanding? This is why scripture says, "Bodhisattvas entering concentration are not yet free of the phenomenon of this concentration."

Scripture also says, "Having realized the purity of the realm of reality by permanent detachment through laborious meditation, that understanding of purity then becomes self-obstruction. You should know there is an even deeper mind."

Tzu-te

The Blind Leading the Blind

There are some white-robed lay devotees who keep up the discipline of not eating after noon as if they were saints, yet are completely wrapped up in profiteering, ruining commoners and kinfolk. When they die, every one of them will be like turtles with their shells stripped off alive, winding up like foxes and badgers skinned alive, going right to uninterrupted hell, to be sunk forever without a break. An ancient said, "When one who is blind leads many who are blind, they lead each other into a pit of fire." The *Scripture of Complete Enlightenment* says, "It is not people's fault, but the error of false teachers."

P'u-an (d. 1169)

This Mind

Bodhidharma came from the West and just pointed to the human mind, to show its nature and enlighten it. That was undeniably direct and economical, but when seen with the absolute eye, it is already all mixed up. There is no choice for now but to make some medicine for a dead horse.

This mind that is simply pointed to is precisely what the Buddha could not express in forty-nine years of lectures and talks. It is extremely rarefied, extremely subtle; few are able to find the true pulse.

This mind cannot be transmitted but can only be experienced in oneself and understood in oneself. When you get to the point where there is neither delusion nor enlightenment, you simply dress and eat as normal, without a bunch of arcane interpretations and lines of doctrine jamming your chest, so you're clear and uncluttered.

Ying-an (d. 1163)

An Inexhaustible Treasury

Correctness in self-management is in the self; the most important step of a thousand-mile journey is the first one. If you manage both of these well, then you have graduated the infinite subtle doctrines of the hundred thousand doors of the teaching. Therefore this is called concentration of an inexhaustible treasury.

Ying-an

The Experience of the True Human Being

The founding teacher came from the West and pointed directly at the human mind to show its nature and foster enlightenment, but in Zen this is like digging a hole in the ground and burying people alive. It was out of temporal necessity that medicine for a dead horse was made, with talk about Buddha, Zen masters, mind, and nature, like switching sweet fruit for bitter gourd.

As for powerful people, they cut in two with one blow of the sword, stepping back into themselves, seeing through to the original face before a single thought is conceived, illuminating the universe, penetrating everywhere. Then they are no different from Shakyamuni Buddha. This is called the crowning royal concentration, it is called the bonfire, it is called the diamond sword, it is called the crouching lion, it is called the poison drum; it is referred to by various names.

At this time, who makes birth and death? Who makes coming and going? Who makes good and bad? Who makes opposition and harmony? Who makes right and wrong? Who makes heaven and hell? Who makes the various states of being? The whole world is a door of liberation; the whole thing is the experience of the true human being with no position.

Ying-an

Moon and Clouds

Comprehending illusion from within enlightenment is like the moon stamping a thousand peaks; wishing for enlightenment from within illusion is like clouds dotting the endless sky.

P'u-an

One True Source

People who have yet to understand use mind to seek mind and make Buddha seek Buddha. They have no prospect of attainment. What they don't realize is that all conscious beings are of the same one true source.

P'u-an

Direct Experience

You must detach from forms and labels before you can learn the way. When your learning reaches the effortless knowledge that is not learned, the path is not a fixed path — the mind itself is the buddha-mind. Maximum capacity becomes accessible; not from formal externals, but experienced directly.

P'u-an

Adepts and Showoffs

Venerable adepts since ancient times worked on this thing until they had passed through to where there is no trouble at all; only then did they dare to take up positions as guides for others. How could they be compared with those today who show off for fame and profit, blinding people with confusion?

Ying-an

Noncompetitiveness

The way the old adepts of ancient times asked about the path was not competitive or contentious; they would inquire of anyone with some strength, even a child. Only thus may people be called students of the way.

Followers of Zen in recent times may say they are going traveling solely to investigate the great concerns of life and death, but though they may imitate the appearances of the ancients, they remain very competitive and contentious. Once you have this problem, the source of direct pointing cannot be understood.

It is like the case of archers: if they start out competing, they'll never achieve good marksmanship. It is after long practice without thought of winning or losing that they can hit the target. So it is with study of the path: if even a single thought of winning and losing abides in the heart, you will be chained by winning and losing.

Ying-an

Understanding

First of all, do not predefine understanding, and do not make a principle of nonunderstanding.

Ying-an

Going Beyond

When you get to the point where even a thousand people, even ten thousand people, cannot trap you or cage you, that is still not expertise. You must go on to the beyond and activate the transcendental key, never injuring your hand against the sharp edge, bringing everyone in the world to life.

Ying-an

Zen and Gender

The transcendental path is not masculine or feminine.

Ying-an

Charlatans

Pay close attention. An ancient worthy said, "A swift hound does not bare its teeth, but hardly do you make a move before it's on you right away!" Students in recent times insist on preaching Zen as religion before they have understood their own selves. They are all charlatans.

Huai-t'ang (twelfth century)

Deterioration

If pilgrims have no spiritual bones, their eyes do not know people, and they do not meet a real true Zen master to open their minds, they plunge into a bag of curios: gathering in groups of two or three hundred, they make wild cries and talk wild talk, discoursing on mind and nature, lecturing on Zen and the way, criticizing and extolling ancients and moderns. They call this Buddhism and consider it the essence of the teaching, but this is actually slandering the universal vehicle, creating seeds of hell.

Such people are very numerous; they are to be pitied. Our path has deteriorated!

Huai-t'ang

The Impassable Barrier

Even if you attain realization of the emptiness of persons and things, this does not measure up to the way of Zen. Even if you embody complete function and complete perception, this is still not the essential wonder of Zen. You must break through the impassable barrier and get to know the opening beyond.

Fo-hsing T'ai (twelfth century)

No Actual Doctrine

If we are to discuss this matter, the simple fact is that there is nothing whatsoever to point out to people. If there were anything at all to indicate to people, Buddhism would not have reached the present day. For this reason the successions of buddhas extending a hand and the successions of Zen masters passing on transmission have done so for lack of practical choice; there has never been an actual doctrine.

Fu-an (twelfth century)

True Speech

The sun may cool off and the moon may heat up, but all the bedevilments there are cannot destroy true speech.

What is true speech? Ninety percent accuracy is not as good as silence.

Yueh-lin (thirteenth century)

Pay Attention

It is presented right to your face, wholeheartedly imparted: if you have keen faculties and higher wisdom, you will carry it with your whole body, with unavoidable strictness. As soon as you get involved in thought, formalizing it in writing and verbal conventions, you have lost contact. Therefore it is said, "The way is nearby, yet you seek it afar."

Just manage to pay attention twenty-four hours a day, whatever you may be doing, stepping back into yourself and silently bringing up over and over again the contemplation "What is this?" Keep contemplating throughout your comings and goings, contemplating until you reach the point where there is no flavor, and no place to get a grip or a foothold, and your body and mind are like space, yet do not seem like space. Suddenly you lose your footing and stomp over the scenery of the original ground, breaking out in a sweat. This makes your life joyful!

Then you can respond to people according to potential, picking up what comes to hand, saying what comes to mind, putting to use what is right there, having a way out in every expression. Buddhism and things of the world become one. Then you go to another genuine teacher to make sure of the profound depths; it is like going into the oceans: the further you go, the deeper it is. The moment there is any clinging, any conceit or dependence on others, you are the same as an outsider. The reason those who study the path in the present time are not as advanced as earlier ones is often because they gain a little and consider it enough.

Sung-yuan (1139–1209)

Quintessential Zen

Since time immemorial, when buddhas or Zen masters have dealt with sharp and clear people with the keen faculties appropriate to the higher vehicle, they have simply required transcendence of feelings, detachment from views, and liveliness of functions, knowing something before it's brought up, understanding something before it's said, cutting through appearances, never pursuing thought in the conceptual faculty, making body and mind empty, immaterially spiritual, serenely sublimated, inwardly clarifying independent individual perception, outwardly unattached to anything at all. When inside and outside are clear, there is only one true reality: not being companion to myriad things, not congregating with the thousand sages, you are independently liberated, transcendent, independent, and free.

Sung-yuan

Self-Obstruction

The essence of the message that is specially transmitted outside of doctrine is present in all states,
and the true mind is in all consciousnesses; the radiant
light of its powers, freedoms, and total functioning
shines brilliantly day and night without interruption.
Yet people do not consciously know it; they make their
own obstructions, blowing it off to the back of their
brains. Then they go elsewhere to ask about Buddha, to
ask about mastery, to seek Zen, to seek the path. For
this reason they are called pitiful.

P'o-an (1136–1211)

Stand on Your Own

Zennists are spontaneously able to roar the lion's roar while still in their mothers' wombs. Only when you are like this can you uphold this school. As for those who are conceited yet rely on others, depending on instructions from another, memorizing the sayings of others as if this were the way to the source, all of them are destroyers of Buddhism.

The fact that this path has not been flourishing in recent times is because teachers and disciples give each other approval and recognition, ignoring cause and effect and duping the people, claiming themselves able to uphold this school. It is like sculpting a "sandal-wood" icon out of dung — no matter how long a time passes, it simply stinks.

You should get away from such people as soon as possible. Apply your own concentrated attention, apply your own eyes and brains; develop yourself, stand on your own. One day your own eyes will clear and will radiate light shining through the whole world. Only then will you live up to the aim of your journey.

When a master craftsman instructs people, he can give them compass and ruler but cannot give them skill. The function of Zen teachers is otherwise: first they take away your compass and ruler, then wait until you can cut squares and circles freehand, spontaneously conforming to compass and ruler; thus the skill is therein.

Even so, this too is a temporary byroad, a little resting place. Going through the gate of Zen, you still have to study for thirty years.

Ch'ih-chueh (fl. ca. 1208–1225)

The Realm of Buddhahood

An ancient said, "If people want to know the realm of buddhahood, they should make their minds clear as open space, detaching from all false thoughts and all grasping, making their minds unobstructed wherever they turn." What is the realm of buddhahood? Basically it is the normal course of one's own mind in everyday life; it's just that one daily buries one's head in things and events and is swept along under the influence of objects.

If you want to harmonize with the realm of buddhahood, if you can just keep mindful twenty-four hours a day, not giving up through every state of mind, one day it will be like meeting an old friend in a busy city: "Oh! So here you are!"

When you get to this state, errant thoughts and all grasping melt right away, and everything becomes your own subtle function.

Ch'ih-chueh

The Failure of Zen

The failure of the Zen path comes from teachers without deep attainment just setting forth sayings and showing off knowledge as a tool to capture students, and from students with no great aspiration just following popular fads and current customs, content to sink themselves in the domain of intellectual knowledge and verbiage, not knowing how to return. The "teachers" and "students" bewitch each other.

Ch'ih-chueh

The Normal Course

The normal course of everyday life is not in events and things; the source not transmitted by a thousand sages is not confined to the realm of mystic wonder. If you don't have your feet on the real ground, with the wonder in the turning point, how are you worth talking to about this?

If in the midst of events and things you see all the way through, then the source not transmitted by a thousand sages appears every moment; if you can shed the realm of mystic wonder, then the normal course of everyday life will fit into the groove.

Ch'ih-chueh

The Mind

How great the mind is! It is so vast it is all-encompassing, so fine it is all-pervading. Enhancement doesn't make excess; minimization doesn't make lack. Silently it operates spontaneously; serenely it responds skillfully. It is swift without speeding; it arrives without going. Location and mass cannot contain it; measurements and numbers cannot plumb it.

It is clearly there in the midst of everyday activities, but students cannot avail themselves of it because emotional thoughts stultify them and desire for gain dulls them. In subtle ways, they are compelled by creation, subsistence, change, and extinction; in crude ways, they are compelled by earth, water, fire, and air. Forgetting themselves, they pursue things; abandoning the real, they pursue the artificial. Ultimately swept away irrevocably, everyone in the world is like this.

If you can get rid of the veils over the mind, restore the root of nature, and clearly see the mind in the midst of everyday life, then emotions, thoughts, and desires; creation, subsistence, change, and extinction; earth, water, fire, and air, are all your own subtle functions.

Ch'ih-chueh

Inside and Outside

"There is no thing before the eyes" — a long sword against the sky. "The idea is before the eyes" — a thousand peals of thunder roar. Whether you get it or not, you still do not escape losing your life.

This matter is so vast it contains the universe, so fine it penetrates atomic particles. It is not comprehended by perception and cognition, not understood by worldly knowledge and intellectual brilliance. Yuan-wu said, "It should not be that it exists when you speak of it but not when you don't." Miao-hsi said, "It cannot be that it is there when you're sitting on a cushion and not there when you get off the meditation seat."

Here, turn over the tongues of these two elders, and then you will know there is a living road right in front of you. Twenty-four hours a day, throughout all of your activities, you "enter the forest without disturbing the grasses, go into the water without stirring up waves." Even in an urban environment, you are not caged or bridled by sound and form; even if prosperous and well positioned, you are not moved or changed by the glory of success. Thus it is said, "Break out from inside, and your power is strong; break in from outside, and your power is weak."

Fo-chih (fl. ca. 1228)

Action and Stillness

Let your actions be like clouds going by; the clouds going by are mindless. Let your stillness be as the valley spirit; the valley spirit is undying. When action accompanies stillness and stillness combines with action, then the duality of action and stillness no longer arises.

Pei-chien (1185–1246)

Discovery of Mind

Teachers have appeared in the world to uphold this thing, spreading a net to bring in those of the very highest capacity. When you find out their essential subtlety, it is not beyond the discovery of each individual's own mind.

Once the mind is clear, this very word *clarity* doesn't stick anywhere anymore; it is like a snowflake on a red-hot fireplace.

When you get to such a state, you still need long-term refinement and polishing to reach complete maturity.

Once the roots are firm, there is no need to worry that the branches might not flourish. Only then can you deal with important matters and take on great responsibilities. Life and death, calamity and fortune, cannot move you at all; whether you are in adversity or prosperity, withdrawn or expansive, in activity or in quietude, you hit the target in every case.

In action, you adapt to changes with intuitive penetration and complete fluidity without bound. In stillness, you are open and clear, independently illumined, not imprisoned by special wondrous states. This is what is meant by the saying "All times and all places are my livelihood."

Wu-chun (d. 1249)

Daily Activities

The path is in daily activities, but if you linger in daily activities, then you are taking a thief for your son. If you seek some special life outside of daily activities, that is like brushing aside waves to look for water.

Wu-chun

The Path and the End

The path cannot be sought — the important thing is just to stop the mind. However, this stopping is not to be forced. You need to search morning and night until you reach the point where the road of conception comes to an end, whereupon you'll suddenly spontaneously stop. After this stopping, the racing and seeking mind stops.

It is like a traveler stopping at an inn. In his desire to get where he's going, he puts his effort into traveling, for if he doesn't travel he won't get there. Once he's arrived, all the toils and pains of the road come to an end and he goes running off no more.

Wu-chun

The Pivot of the Zen Gate

The pivot of the Zen gate is not a matter of going from group to group; how does the guiding principle of Zen seekers need taking on one teacher after another?

If you see horns on the other side of a fence, clearly there's an inference to be made. If you still want to depict it in words, that's like the case of a master painter making a lifelike portrait of an ox — after all it's not a live ox.

I have heard that the verbal teachings of the Zen masters are for orienting the efforts of people of the time: if their efforts are not disoriented, don't bother to orient them. The verbal teachings of Zen masters and buddhas are prescriptions for curing the insane; if the mind and spirit are not deranged, don't bother to cure them.

The only words to be said to those who know are *urgency* and *intentness*. If you don't clearly understand your own self, you have no way to fend off birth and death; if you do not understand the surroundings, how can you tell right from wrong?

Chueh-an (1250s)

Worldly Affairs

Men of affairs who are in positions of wealth and rank yet are not trapped by wealth and rank, and are also able to break through the iron face of the mortal being and focus their minds on this path, must already have the seed of wisdom; otherwise, how could they reach this?

The trouble is not being able to do real true work in deadly earnest. We see many who think and compare, consciously anticipating enlightenment, trying deliberately to achieve cessation, rejoicing when others privately acknowledge them, wanting people to praise them. As soon as you give rise to these thoughts, this is the root of birth and death.

Hsi-sou (fl. ca. 1249)

Awaken on Your Own

Learning the path of Zen study has no special mysterious gateway or essential road: it requires individuals to awaken on their own. If you have awakened correctly once, you see mountains are not mountains and rivers are not rivers; then after that you see mountains are mountains and rivers are rivers. If you are not awakened, when you see things you are obstructed by seeing, influenced by things, confused by objects. This is what is called restlessness of habit-ridden consciousness, in which there is no reliable basis.

Yun-ku (fl. ca 1256)

The Great Way

The great way is right before our eyes, but it is still hard to see what is right before our eyes. If you want to know the true substance of the great way, it is not apart from sound and form, words and speech.

Wu-men (1183–1260)

Buddhism and Human Sentiment

Even if one's body is wrapped in hot iron, and molten copper is poured down one's throat, one should never equate Buddhism with human sentiment.

When human sentiments are thick, the sense of truth is slight. What does the world know of true capacities and human sentiments? Where there are only vain human sentiments, there is no real capacity; how long can human sentiments last?

Wu-men

Thorough Cooking

Once three scholars on the way to the civil service examination stopped to buy refreshments from a woman who sold pastries by the wayside. One man was calm and quiet, while the other two argued over literature. The woman asked where they were going. The latter two told her they were going to take the civil service examination. She said, "You two scholars won't pass the exam; that other man will." The two men swore at her and left.

When the results of the examination turned out as the woman had predicted, the two scholars who had failed went back to find out how she had known they would not pass, while the third man would. They asked her if she knew physiognomy. "No," she said, "all I know is that when a pastry is thoroughly cooked, it sits there quietly, but before it's finished it keeps on making noise."

Wu-men

Nominal Zen Study

Master Shih-t'ou said, "A thousand kinds of sayings and ten thousand sorts of explanations are just intended to teach you to always be unconfused." What is popular in groups nowadays is just nominal Zen study; to try to find even one person who is always unconfused is like trying to pick the moon from the sky.

Tuan-ch'iao (ca. 1241)

Life and Death

The matter of life and death is important; impermanence is swift. Aspirants to Zen all understand the path, but when you ask them why we live and why we die, ten out of ten are dumbstruck. If you go on this way, even if you journey throughout the whole world, what will it accomplish?

Tuan-ch'iao

Daily Activities

The way is in daily activities; it is used every day, unknowingly. That is why it is said, "Knowing is false consciousness, not knowing is indifference." At this point, tell me, is knowing right or is not knowing right?

The elders since time immemorial and the pilgrims all over the world have all scraped through the bottoms of their rice bags and worn out their footgear, but I have never seen anyone who could get through this double barrier.

If you can't get through, it's better to just walk when walking, just sit when sitting.

Hsueh-yen (fl. ca. 1253)

Clarifying Mind

What is most essential to Buddhism is based on clarifying the mind. If you want your mind to be clear, it is important to put opinions to rest. If opinions are not stopped, then wrong and right are confused; if the mind is not clear, reality and illusion are mixed up. If you stop opinions and clear the mind, then reality and illusion are both empty, wrong and right do not stand.

Hsueh-yen

Three Types of Learning

The Buddhist path has its source in the three types of learning — discipline, concentration, and insight. Discipline holds the mind with regulations, concentration illumines the mind with stillness, insight clarifies the mind with wisdom.

If one has insight without concentration or discipline, then one remains unrestrained, uselessly engaging in verbalization without being able to stop repetitive routines and shed birth and death.

If one has concentration without discipline or insight, then one remains in empty stillness and uselessly lingers in blank emptiness and cannot elucidate the great teaching to guide people.

If one has discipline but no concentration or wisdom, then one continues clinging, uselessly getting mired in rules, unable to unify right and wrong and equalize others and self.

Nevertheless, insight is concentration, and concentration is discipline: discipline can produce concentration, concentration can produce insight.

Insight, concentration, and discipline originate in one mind. If the mind fundamentally does not exist, where do discipline, concentration, and insight come from?

So it exists without existing, vast as cosmic space: all

worlds of the whole universe, all the plants, trees, and forests, the birds, beasts, and people, as well as the eighty-four thousand troubles of the world, are all none other than this mind.

When the mind is not aroused, this is discipline; when the mind is unmoved, this is concentration; when the mind is not obscured, this is insight.

Hsueh-yen

The Eyes for the Journey

To journey, you must have eyes for the journey; if you don't have eyes, the old baldies sitting in carved wood chairs everywhere will set out used furniture from the past before you, putting big prices on them, boasting in a hundred ways that they are rare and marvelous treasures. You may lose your eyes and brains all at once; unable to get anywhere, you may not avoid being confused by them and getting into a bunch of antique curios, never to emerge.

Hsi-yen (1198–1262)

Where Is the Problem?

When people spend ten or twenty years, or even a whole lifetime, just clarifying this matter, detached from the world and forgetful of objects, and yet they do not penetrate through to freedom, where is the problem? Genuine seekers should try to bring it out.

Is it lack of spiritual potential? Is it not having met an enlightened teacher? Is it inconsistency? Is it inferiority of faculties and weakness of will? Is it floating and sinking in mundane toils? Is it settling in emptiness and stagnating in stillness? Is it that miscellaneous poisons have gotten into the mind? Is it that the time has not yet arrived? Is it failure to wonder about sayings? Is it that they think they have attained what they have not, or think they have realized what they have not?

Kao-feng (1260s)

The Fire of Zen

This thing is like an enormous fire, fierce flames pervading the sky, with never the slightest interruption. Everything in the world is thrown into it, immediately evaporating away like a fleck of snow.

Kao-feng

Turning Doctrine into Sickness

Those who have spent ten or twenty years brushing aside the weeds looking for the way and yet have not seen the buddha nature often say they are trapped by oblivion and excitement. What they don't realize is that the substance of this very oblivion and excitement is itself buddha nature.

It is a pity that deluded people do not understand; they arbitrarly cling to doctrines and turn them into sicknesses, using sickness to attack sickness. They make it so they get further estranged from buddha nature the more they seek it. The more they hurry, the more they're delayed.

Even if one or two turn their attention around, look back into themselves and realize their error, empty out and forget both medicine and disease so that their eyes emerge and they clearly understand the simple message of Zen, seeing into their original buddha nature, in my estimation this is still something on the shore of birth and death. If you would talk about the road of transcendence, you should know it is even beyond the green mountains.

Kao-feng

Don't Cling to the Cushion

It is essential in Zen study that you do not cling to a sitting cushion for practice. If you sink into oblivion or distraction, or plunge into ease and tranquillity, totally unawares, not only will you waste time, you will not be able to digest the offerings of donors. When the light of your eyes falls to the ground one day, in the end what will you rely on?

Kao-feng

The Inexhaustible Treasury

This matter is like a pile of trash under the eaves of someone's house; from morning to night rain beats on it, wind blows on it, but nobody pays attention to it. They do not realize there is an inexhaustible treasure trove within it; if they could avail themselves of it, they could take from it and put it to use for a hundred aeons and a thousand lifetimes without exhausting it.

You should know that this treasury doesn't come from outside; it all emerges from your faith. If you can have complete faith in it, you certainly won't be cheated. If you do not have complete faith, you will never realize it even in countless aeons. So I ask you to have faith in this way, so you can avoid being destitute beggars.

But tell me, where is this treasury right now?

If you don't go into the tiger's den, how can you catch a tiger cub?

Kao-feng

The Limit of Effort

When you investigate this matter, the extreme limit of effort is like planting flowers in the sky or fishing for the moon in the water: there is simply no place for you to set about it, no place to apply your mind. Time and again people beat the drum of retreat as soon as they run into this state; they don't realize that this is actually news of getting home.

If they are bold, people face the state where there's no place to set to work, when the mind cannot be applied, like great generals in the midst of huge armies, directly capturing their adversaries, mindless of gain or loss. If you truly have such a grasp of the essential, and such keenness, you can achieve success in a fingersnap, attaining sagehood instantly.

Kao-feng

Three Barriers

The bright sun is in the sky, shining on everything; why is it blocked by a cloud?

Everyone has a shadow, which never leaves; why can't you step on it?

The whole world is a fire pit; attaining what state of mind can you avoid being burned?

Kao-feng

Study the Living Word

If you want to reach this state, you should immediately get rid of your previous learned understanding, both that which is clear and that which is obscure, gradually making your whole body like a hot iron ball, next door to death: take up a saying of an ancient and toss it in front of you, looking at it like a born enemy. Day and night be as if you were sitting in thorns, and someday you will naturally have a breakthrough.

Do not under any circumstances stick to the form of sitting. When you do sit, you must employ expedient means; if you do it without inner mastery, you belabor your spirit in vain. An ancient said, "When the mind is vacant and the surroundings are still, it is just because of stagnation. When you study Zen, you should study the living word, not the dead word. If you understand through the dead word, you cannot even save yourself."

Hsu-t'ang (1185–1269)

The Scenery of the Original Ground

The scenery of the original ground is completely fluid and without bounds before mortals and buddhas are there; suddenly it is obscured by false perceptions, whereupon we stagnate and sink into mundane toils, grasping all objects, until we are infected by psychological afflictions. If you are unable to turn attention around to illumine the self right away, how can you pass through so many myriad entanglements?

Whether in adverse or favorable situations, neither grasp nor cling; cut right through speech and silence, being and nothingness, action and stillness. When dealing with things, responding to potentials, like a flying sword discus, like a blazing fire, you leave no shadow or trace at all. Thus you are empty and spiritual, tranquil and sublime; with one perception you illumine myriad distinctions, a thousand differentiations. Arriving directly at a state of great peace, you find there is no stagnation at all.

Hai-yin (ca. 1282)

Fuifillment

Virtue has no fixed teacher — focus on goodness is the teacher. If teachers are effective, then you know they are to be regarded as teachers.

You find out the truth and fulfill your nature to arrive at your destiny; to transcend at once, without going through a process, you need to find out the ultimate.

A monk asked Chao-chou, "Does a dog have buddha nature or not?" Chao-chou said, "No." This is not "no" meaning nonexistence of an existence, nor is it "no" meaning pure nonexistence. It is a nonrational mystic razor, a sublime method of transforming life's fortunes.

Go right ahead and bring it up; right away you'll empty out. Like a silver mountain, an iron wall, you'll be impervious to gain and loss, praise and blame; neither honor nor censure, neither pain nor pleasure, can trap you.

You do not plunge into the sentiments of the ordinary, nor do you fall into the understanding of the sage. Empty and spiritual, serene and sublime, you do not tarry anywhere but attain fulfillment everywhere.

At this time, you should know there is a final statement; only then are you a mature person. Completing the task of the mature person is called transcending the world in the midst of the world, highest of all.

Hai-yin

Delusion and Enlightenment

When deluded, you are deluded about the contents of enlightenment; when enlightened, you are enlightened about the contents of delusion. When delusion and enlightenment are both forgotten, it is like a man cutting off his own head: if his head is cut off, there's no one to do the cutting.

If you see this clearly, right away you'll have no second thought. An ancient said, "Clearly, clearly there is no enlightenment; if there is any dogma, it is delusion." When you get here, you can't take a stand and you can't stay: if you take a stand you will be in peril; if you stay, you will be blind.

Just do not react automatically to the outside world, and do not take refuge in voidness within. Do not pursue trivialities outside, and do not stay in trance inside.

It is imperative that ideas do not inhibit mystery, expressions do not inhibit ideas, and functions do not inhibit potentials. Once these three things are clear, they naturally appear everywhere without need for concentration, naturally clear everywhere without need for special attention.

In this state, frequently meeting is not intimacy, transcendent aloofness is not estrangement. When dealing with them accordingly, one is not obstructed by events; when sitting quietly, one is not lost in the noumenon. Being the master wherever one may be, one finds the source in everything, appearing and disappearing, now reserved, now expansive, having attained great freedom.

And yet one must also know there is an opening beyond.

Hai-yin

Expedients

"Faith is the basis of the path, the mother of virtue; it nourishes all roots of goodness."

Every word uttered by sages of yore as expedient methods were medicines given in accordance with particular ailments — when was there ever any actual dogma to bind people?

If you are confused, there are a thousand differentiations, ten thousand distinctions. If you are enlightened, everything is the same one family.

Wu-chien (fl. ca. 1265–1300)

Directed Effort

Unexcelled sublime enlightenment is originally inherent in everyone, but because of accumulated ages of arbitrary ideas and clinging attachments, people cannot clarify the scenery of the original state all at once. People of great strength should employ real true directed effort, bringing up an ancient saying in all situations, secretly evoking it without interruption through successive states of mind. When you suddenly break through the feeling of doubt, for the first time you will have some freedom.

Wu-chien

Liberation and Blockage

The ancients circulate verbal teachings of buddhas and Zen masters for the edification of later learners, with the subtlety to pull out nails, remove stakes, dissolve stickiness, and remove bonds. When it came to taking care of details over and over, making unconventional changes for effectiveness, they were like rolling round boulders down mountains ten miles high. Perpetuating such examples among those of later ages was for no other reason than to remove mental clinging, contentiousness, intellectual opinion, and theoretical understanding, to place people in the empty and clear, clean and naked, bare and untrammeled state of great liberation.

Now it is otherwise. There tend to be those who are blocked by worldly knowledge and intellectual sharpness, divided into those who argue forcefully and those who overcome themselves; and there are ascetics who fall into quietism or ambitious activism. When you observe their behavior, they all claim to have the claws and fangs of time immemorial, but when it comes to situational adaptation in contact with conditions at large, they are invariably living in ghost caves in mountains of darkness.

This matter is certainly not to be rushed. It is essential that the individual be clear and precise in getting the gist, and after that not leak at all twenty–four hours a day. Only then is it appropriate to go to another for certain discernment, lest one still be blown by the wind of intellectual understanding. If one is unwilling to give up what one has treasured, it will become a serious problem in the future.

Even more problematic is when one wants to clarify this matter without a genuine basis and without the necessary attainments. How is that different from worms dancing in hopes of soaring into the misty clouds and undergoing a miraculous transformation? Can they do it?

Ku-lin (fl. ca. 1297–1308)

Nameless and Traceless

When mind does not stick to things and consciousness does not dwell in mystery, great knowledge is nameless, true emptiness is traceless. So where do you place your feet twenty-four hours a day? If you are immediately unconcerned, you fall into perception and cognition; yet as soon as you get into deliberate arrangement, you do not escape dependence and attachment.

Ku-lin

Collecting Conversation Pieces

Fen-yang called on more than seventy teachers: only one or two had insight and vision; the rest were nothing to talk about. Recently there are some people whose knowledge is not clear and who have not learned their own fundamental task; unable to make an existential investigation, instead they work from books, trying to get a supply of things to talk about. They are mistaken — they have thrown away real gold to go after rubble.

Ku-lin

Total Zen

Zen is your original face; there is no special Zen to study other than this. And there is nothing to see or hear either — the totality of this seeing and hearing is Zen; outside of Zen, no other seeing or hearing can be found.

Ming-pen (1263–1323)

A Method of Stopping

Zen is the teaching of the true ground of mind. If you are sure you want to comprehend the great matter of life and death, you should know that with a single thought of doubt or confusion you fall into the realm of demons.

When you are concentrating, if your thoughts are mixed up, and random ideas are in a jumble, don't mind them at all, regardless of whether they're good or bad, true or false. Just turn to a saying, until you reach the point where as soon as you resort to the saying it stops torpor, distraction, and miscellaneous thoughts flying in confusion. After a long time of this, they will spontaneously stop.

Even if they don't stop, you still don't need to forcibly suppress them; just keep concentrated right mindfulness continuous, and that's all. If concentrated right mindfulness is stable and continuous, thoughts will naturally dissolve. When thoughts dissolve, then there is hope of transcendent realization of sudden enlightenment.

Once you have attained enlightenment, you will naturally have insight: it can be said that in your own mind you will naturally comprehend the near future, the distant future, what is false and what is not false,

and whether there are so many great and small awak-
enings. You won't need to ask anyone else.

If you haven't awakened yet, for now do not idly
ponder this trivia — it will only increase your torpor
and distraction.

Ming-pen

Turning Attention around to Look Within

Turning the attention around to look within is the domain of independent liberation from ordinary sentiments and transcendent access to the realm of great enlightenment. If your work has not yet reached this state, how is attention turned around? How does one look within?

If you have not yet arrived at the stage of true enlightenment, if there is any theory of turning around or introspection, it is all self-deception. When you are thoroughly enlightened, the light of mind turns around without depending on being turned around, awareness introspects without depending on being introverted.

Because there is no dependence, there is no light to turn around and no looking to direct within. This is called absorption in one practice. The buddhas and Zen masters have all dug in their heels here — it is quite unattainable by conceptual consciousness and emotional illusion.

Nowadays some ignoramuses go to quiet, isolated places and gather in their looking and listening, cutting off seeing and hearing, so that they are like wood or stone, and they call that turning the attention around and looking within. They can go on "looking" this way for thirty years, wishing every moment to shed birth and death, but they will not succeed.

Ming-pen

Looking into a Saying

Just believe in yourself, and bring up the saying you are looking into. Keep on looking into it no matter how long it takes, and you will naturally penetrate someday. While you are looking into it, don't give rise to any doubtful thinking, and don't give rise to any hurry for enlightenment.

When you are doing the work looking into a saying, whatever extraordinary marvels or effects you may perceive or experience, these are all bedeviling entanglements; as long as you do not let your mind pursue them, they will eventually dissolve of themselves. If you suddenly conceive a momentary feeling of enjoyment or attachment, from this you will fall into the realm of bedevilment. You may think you've awakened, but actually you're deranged.

Enlightenment is like someone returning home: everything is familiar, so one is naturally comfortable and clear about everything, without any further thoughts of doubt or confusion at all. If there is still half a speck of doubt or confusion, it certainly isn't your home. Then you must toss it away and seek elsewhere; otherwise you'll get conceited and develop idiosyncratic views.

Ming-pen

No Arrangement

Mind is originally clear and calm, fundamentally free from pollution; and there is no difference between doing and not doing concentration. In all activities it is only essential to understand one's own mind clearly.

This mind does not come under any arrangement at all; it must be experienced by realization. If it is not realized by way of authentic enlightenment, whatever the myriad mystical understandings or thousand kinds of thoughts you may have, you are "like someone trying to rub space with your hands." How can you apprehend the body of space for you to rub?

Míng-pen

Reality and Imitations

It is imperative to speak according to reality and act according to reality; only that constitutes harmonization.

We regularly see Zen teachers of recent times teaching people to bring up a saying: "Myriad things return to one; where does one return?" They also teach people to contemplate this story: A monk asked Chao-chou, "Does a dog have buddha nature or not?" Chao-chou said, "No." They make them come for interrogation morning and evening, and keep them wondering, calling this great doubt, necessitating great enlightenment. Although this is a clever expedient for a period of time, nevertheless it has added increased obstruction.

On this acount, complete ignoramuses have disguised themselves as Zen monks: they don't know the scriptural teachings, don't keep the precepts, and are utterly at a loss when questoned; they just say they have asked for instruction from a teacher. Bringing up a saying, they recite it and think about it, like a village school teaching children to repeat after an adult. While they're awake they remember, then when they fall asleep they forget. Some concentrate too hard, and become more confused the more they doubt, eventually reaching the point where they lose their minds and go crazy.

Some fabricate prognostications, saying strange things to deceive and threaten the ignorant. Some spend their whole lives in unknowing quietism in a ghost cave in a mountain of blackness, never attaining the slightest empowerment. They still don't realize that it's like an ox drawing a cart; if the cart isn't moving, do you hit the cart or the ox?

Also, Buddha said that if you cling to anything, this is called conceptual attachment, whereby you fall into the notion of permanence; but if you are totally mindless, that is called naturalism, fallen into a nihilistic view.

Hsiao-yin (fl. ca. 1330)

Sharp but Inconspicuous

To learn this path it is important to be sharp yet inconspicuous. When you are sharp, you are not confused by people; when you are inconspicuous, you don't contend with people. Not being confused by people, you are empty and spiritual; not contending with people, you are serene and subtle.

Liao-an (fl. ca 1330)

Functions of Zen

Zen is a razor to cut off birth and death; Zen is a bodkin to undo knots; Zen is a mirror to distinguish the beautiful and the ugly; Zen is a sword to cut off error and delusion; Zen is an axe to cut down a forest of brambles; Zen is a strategy for defeating enemies; Zen is a basis for attaining enlightenment and exercising mastery.

Liao-an

No Dogma

When the ancients uttered a word or half a phrase, it was to resolve sticking points, untie bonds, pull out nails, and remove stakes; how could they have had any dogma to bind people? We see many students who cling to the pointing finger, taking it for the moon; they seek mystery and marvel, they seek intellectual understanding, instead of a way to the source. They are to be deeply pitied.

So for people of superior faculties and keen insight, this matter is not hard to see. As for those of lesser potential and capacity who are also lazy and pursue trivia in neglect of the fundamental, they have no hope of attainment. In reality, they exclude themselves.

Liao-an

Beyond Measure

The essence of mind is unpolluted, basically complete in itself. Just detach from false mental objects and there is the Buddha of being as is.

When deluded, you deviate from the real and pursue the false; when enlightened, you abandon the false and return to the real.

After you have reached the point where reality and falsehood both melt and delusion and enlightenment lodge nowhere, then you use up your old karma according to conditions, trusting essence and enjoying natural reality, exercising kindness and compassion, helping out the orphaned and the unsheltered, forgetting subject and object, annihilating shadow and form, becoming a person beyond measure, living in a realm of experience beyond measure, and doing a task beyond measure.

Liao-an

Curing Madness

The teachings of the whole vast canon are all prescriptions for curing the mad. If you see through the origin, the mad mind abruptly stops, and you may spontaneously burst out in a laugh.

Liao-an

The Fundamental

Just get the fundamental, don't worry about the out-growths. What is the root, what are the out-growths? Knowing the mind and seeing its essence is the root; explaining Zen and expounding the path are outgrowths. If you know the mind and see its essence, you may speak at will and go where your feet take you — nothing is not the path.

Liao-an

Mistaking a Thief for Your Son

"People studying the way do not know the real simply because they have been acknowledging the conscious mind. The root of infinite aeons of birth and death, ignorant people call it the original human being." If learners do not distinguish skillfully, and mistake the conscious mind for the self, this is what is referred to in the teachings as taking a thief for one's son — the family fortune will never be established.

Liao-an

A Place to Start

If beginners studying Zen fear they have as yet no place to start and no direction, even so, there's nothing else to say but that you each have an original face, which you have never recognized. This original face is one with all buddhas: twenty-four hours a day, as you are speaking, silent, active, quiet, walking, standing, sitting, and lying down, all of this is due to its empowerment. Just recognize this inwardly, and there you have a place to start; there you have direction.

Wei-tse (d. 1348)

The Subtle Path

The subtle path of buddhas and Zen masters is not an irrational creation of knotty problems, nor is it eccentricity or weirdery. And it is not something that is very lofty and hard to practice: it is just what you presently use all the time in your everyday activities. If we have to give it a name, we might call it the natural real Buddha in your own nature, or the master within your own self.

In everyday terms, at all times and in all places, you see and hear with Shakyamuni Buddha's eyes and ears, you speak and breathe with Zen founder Bodhidharma's tongue and nose. In ultimate terms, the individual lives of all the buddhas and Zen masters of the ten directions are all in your grip — whether to gather them together or let them disperse is all up to you.

Wei-tse

Awareness Itself

The subtle, perfect essence of awareness is basically spontaneously open and calm, equanimous and pure, vast as space. It cannot be pointed out in terms of any concrete form, it cannot be approached in terms of location. It cannot be entered into by any door or road, it cannot be depicted or copied by the colors of the spectrum.

Wei-tse

Stopping and Seeing

"Calmness and insight develop through stilling thoughts: the mind of the buddhas manifests therein." This saying seems to refer to cessation and observation, or stopping and seeing.

The ocean of nature to which all things alike return is essentially united, quiet, always clear and calm. When it is stirred by the influences of conditions, then billows of consciousness and waves of emotion well up in ten thousand ways. If not for stopping, there is no way to clarify its clarity and calm its calmness.

The cosmos of reality completely manifesting unity is always evident and always clear when views are gone and things disappear: as soon as it is obscured by the dust of behavioral and intellectual obstructions, then the fog of confusion and clouds of delusion coalesce into myriad forms. If not for seeing, there is no way to bring to light its evident clarity.

When all agitations have ceased and not a single wave arises, myriad phenomena are clear, without confusion, without obstruction. Thus seeing is not separate from stopping. Once the layers of obscurity have been cleared and no clouding occurs, the ten directions are empty, without stirring, without agitation. Thus stopping is not outside of seeing.

Stopping is like concentration, seeing is like insight.

Insofar as we see by stopping, concentration is the catalyst of insight; insofar as we stop by seeing, insight is the basis of concentration. When the catalyst of insight does not run dry, stopping is sufficient to assist the function of seeing; when the basis of concentration is not lacking, seeing is adequate to fulfill the achievement of stopping.

Stopping without seeing may deteriorate into stagnation; seeing without stopping may degenerate into inquisitiveness. Stopping is of course stopping motion, but it is also the root of motion: so when stopping without seeing, one either falls into empty quiescence, or distraction arises. Seeing is of course illumining the obscure, but it is also the root of obscurity: so when seeing without stopping, either one drifts into thought and reflection, or immersion in illusion occurs. Therefore stopping and seeing need each other; neither one can be neglected.

So this stopping is not intrinsic stopping: it depends on motion and stillness to manifest its achievement. And this seeing is not independent seeing: it depends on obscurity and clarity to reveal its function. Since they are not beyond achievement and function, how can they be called true stopping and true seeing?

If stopping and achievement are not set up, and seeing and function are both forgotten, after that both motion and stillness are stopping with true seeing, and both darkness and light are seeing with true stopping.

When stopping with true seeing merges motion and

stillness, then the hundreds of thousands of buddhas enter into right concentration in the midst of billows of feeling and waves of consciousness, which do not harm that which is essentially unified and silent. When seeing with true stopping merges darkness and light, then the eighty thousand methods of practice illumine right knowledge in the midst of the fog of confusion and clouds of illusion, which do not inhibit that which causes views to vanish and things to disappear.

When you get to this, then thoughts become still without being stilled, calmness and insight arise without being produced, the mind of the buddhas appears without being revealed. To try to liken it to the body of cosmic space or the light of a thousand suns would be to be further away than the sky is from the earth.

Wei-tse

The Great Way

People who study the path today do not understand the great way — they only strive to fulfill greed and ambition. At the very outset of their inspiration to study the way, their initial understanding is already mistaken.

The way is the path of fundamental purity: for immense aeons, and even up to the present day, it has no gain or loss, no new or old, no light or dark, no form or name. It is not more in the buddhas and not less in ordinary people. To insist on calling it the way is already defiling; to say something is accomplished by methods of learning the way is what I have called mistaken. It was for lack of choice that the ancients referred to people heading for transcendence as students of the way. The study is that there is nothing to study; the way is that there is nothing to be a way. Since there is nothing to study, there is no clinging; since there is nothing to be a way, there is no following. If one idly slips and says the word *Buddha*, one must simply wash out one's mouth for three years — only thus can one be called a real student of the way.

Nan-ch'uan said, "The way is not in the province of knowing, nor in the province of unknowing. Knowing is false consciousness, unknowing is indifference. If you truly arrive at the way without doubt, it is like cosmic space — how can you insist on affirmation and denial?"

Shu-chung (d. 1386)

The Original Face

What was my original face before my parents gave birth to me? This *kung-an* is a sharp sword for cutting through the net of birth and death, a giant axe for felling the tree of afflictions. Just look into it closely at all times, whatever you are doing, never forgetting it for a moment. After a long time at this, it will naturally become unmixed, coming up spontaneously without being brought up, coming to mind spontaneously without being brought to mind: from head to heels, the whole body is just this one saying.

When you get to this point, you cannot even find any arising of previous mundane toils and false ideas. Suddenly the bottom falls out of the bucket of lacquer, before and after are cut off; then you will attain realization.

Even so, there is still a final revelation.

Nan-shih (fl. ca 1368–1425)

Real Truth

Generally speaking, on this path it is important to work on real truth. When real truth stamps the mind, the path becomes self-evident. If the mind is not true, then even if you attend lectures every day and discuss the path constantly, this just provides topics of conversation and is ultimately of no benefit on the path.

So what is real truth? It is just a matter of looking back into the purity of your own mind in the course of daily activities, not being influenced by anything wrong. That is because mind is like a monkey, consciousness like a horse: without the chain and bridle of great awareness watching them, it will be truly hard to control them no matter how clever your devices.

But when you have whipped and thrashed them into submission, so they merge back into oneness, and all traces of birth and extinction disappear, then you naturally realize basic subtle illumination, thoroughly empty yet uncannily penetrating and effective.

Actuality itself is mind — there is nothing extra. Speech and action both accord with perfect objectivity. Only then can it be said that you are not deceiving your mind.

When you reach the point of not deceiving your

175

mind, then all things, whether mundane or transcendental, are Buddha teachings; whether it is aroused or unaroused, your mind is the buddha mind.

Hui-ching (1528–1598)

Genuine Seekers

Genuine seekers of true enlightenment should first question themselves and discover their inherent spiritual light. Then they must meet others to find out the handle of going beyond. As they penetrate the subtle crux of being and nonbeing, grasping and rejecton are both empty; as they pass through the dark machinations of gain and loss, they devote no energy to matters of glory and disgrace.

Hui-ching

Clarity and Calmness

When stopping and seeing have no entryways, then oblivion and distraction are used for doors. When oblivion and distraction have no ground, clarity and calmness are the sources. Thus those who travel the way unfailingly make skillful use of the fire of stopping and seeing to burn off the dross of oblivion and distraction. Once the refinement is complete, the essence of stopping and seeing becomes concentration and insight.

Thus sages may overturn heaven and earth without being disturbed; this is the power of concentration. They make penetrating investigation into all things without getting confused; this is the efficacy of insight.

If this is so, then in ordinary people clarity and calm are oblivion and distraction, while in sages oblivion and distraction are concentration and insight.

Tzu-po (1543–1604)

Discovering the Light of Mind

Beginners learning the way should make their will firm and strong: twenty-four hours a day, wield the sword of positive energy to overcome demons and curses, cutting off psychological afflictions. When you look into a saying continuously, you spontaneously discover the light of mind, containing heaven and earth, every land completely revealed.

Chien-ju (1549–1619)

Two Tests

I have tested people by means of two things, and have never yet seen anyone pass through. What are these two things? One is testing them by writings. These writings are the body of teachings consisting of the sayings of the buddhas. If you say you have experienced realization, this must be realization of your own mind. One's own mind is itself the buddha mind; if you have realized the buddha mind, you should understand the words of buddhas. If you understand the words of buddhas, then you must be able to immediately understand the teachings of the scriptures expounded by the buddhas, as well as the diverse stories of the Zen masters, without doubt or confusion. If any have doubts, then their claims of realization are not necessarily so.

The second thing is testing the mind in the course of daily activities and interactions. There seem to be some who act as masters to some extent, to whom people resort, but they are not really enlightened. But leaving them aside, what about when in tranquil quietude detached from things, or while sitting in meditation; there seems to be something there, going up and down — that is, right and wrong, gain and loss, doubt and confusion, grasping and rejecting. Can you be at peace? If you are at peace, then even if every plant and tree in the world turned into a human being, each with infinite tongues, with countless challenging questions of infinite complexity on every tongue, all posed simultaneously, it would only require a fingersnap to answer them all. That would be considered attainment of great confidence and freedom.

If you are as yet unable to be at peace, not only are you unable to interact with keen liveliness — even when you are at rest with nothing to do you are already mixed up. Therefore it is said, "For others to approve me is easy; for me to approve myself is hard."

Yuan-cheng (ca. 1570s–1620s)

Pure Eyes

Learners use the teachings of the canon to open their own pure eyes; if one's own eyes are fundamentally pure, what is the need to open them any further? The teachings are expounded for those who have not understood. The *Scripture of Complete Enlightenment* says, "Buddhahood is only attained after permanent cessation of ignorance by means of purity of panoramic awareness." If you know that ignorance is originally nonexistent and the nature of consciousness is unreal, then mountains and rivers do not block the light of your eyes — how can senses and objects damage the body of awareness? Seeing through countless worlds does not seem hard.

Yuan-lai (1575–1630)

Natural Real Buddha Nature

The natural real buddha nature is always inherently complete and luminous; it was thus before our parents gave birth to us, it is thus right now, and it will always be thus forever.

Originally there is not a single thing. Since there's not a single thing, what is to be called original? If you can see into this, you will save the most mental energy.

When divergent thoughts arise, adamantly cut them off yourself. This is expediently called concentration and insight, but it is not a reality; this mind itself is inherently concentrated and inherently insightful.

Huang-po said, "This mind is always intrinsically round and bright, illuminating everywhere. People of the world don't know it, and just recognize perception and cognition as mind. Empty perception and cognition, and the road of mind comes to an end." He also said, "If you want to know the mind, it is not apart from perception and cognition; and yet the original mind does not belong to perception and cognition either."

When you come to this, it is really essential for you to look into yourself; it is not a matter of verbal explanation. The more the talk, the further removed from the way. Those who are successful at introspection know for themselves when the time comes and do not need to ask anyone — all false imaginations and emotional thoughts naturally disappear. This is the effect of learning the way.

A thousand falsehoods do not compare to a single truth. If you are not thus, even if you consciously apply your mind, seeking effectiveness daily, it is all in the realm of impermanence, becoming and passing away. A master teacher said, "If you want to cultivate practice and seek to become a buddha, I don't know where you will try to seek the real." If you can see reality within the mind spontaneously, having reality is the basis of attaining buddhahood. If you seek Buddha externally without seeing your own essential nature, you are an utter ignoramus.

Ta-tu (seventeenth century)

The Spiritual Light

"The spiritual light shines independently, transcendentally liberated from organs and objects of sense." This statement has said it all. If you can understand this, how could I presume to talk a lot? If you can't, then I'll go on and make some complications for now.

The spiritual light of living beings originally has no obstruction, yet deluded feelings arise in confusion. From this there are six sense organs within and objects of the six senses outside: with the opposition of organs and objects, false consciousness arises uncontrolled, producing good and bad, initiating virtuous and evil actions. Because of these actions, living beings revolve in a variety of mundane states, like a pulley wheel, wave after wave, age after age, emerging and sinking, with no end to it. The buddhas took pity on them and expounded the great teaching to them, all just to clarify this independent shining of spiritual light.

If the spiritual light is not obscured, organs and objects suddenly disappear, mind is forgotten, and the world is silent: panoramic awareness all-embracing, the substance of awakening is being as is.

If the light is not revealed, you need a method. The method is not asking someone to explain, it is not studying scriptures, it is not doing a lot of charitable acts, it is not closing the eyes and sitting as if dead. Just look intently into the question of what your original face is in the course of daily life. Don't think about whether it is hard or easy, or remote or near; and don't worry that your own faculties and potential are slow and dull, or that you are too heavily obstructed by past habits. Just go right ahead and do it; after a long time, eventually you will bump into it all of a sudden.

Yuan-hsien (1618–1697)

Effort in Study

Everyone has a torch giving off great light: originally it spontaneously illumines heaven and earth; there is no distance to which it does not reach. It is no different from the buddhas and Zen masters, but when it gets covered by false ideas and material toils, so that it cannot come out, it is therefore necessary to use effort in study to polish it.

What is effort in study? It means placing your everyday mental and physical energies on one saying, without allowing any deviation. After a long time, not only will your mental and physical energies congeal into one mass; the whole earth, mountains and rivers, and the space of the ten directions will also congeal into a single mass, like an iron pill.

One day, through some chance event, the iron pill will explode, producing the eyes of Zen; then the mountains, rivers, and whole earth are all one vast treasury of light.

Yuan-hsien

Participation

The path of Zen values participation. What participation means is that it cannot be ordered by teachers and elders, it cannot be done for you by colleagues, it cannot be adulterated by external energies, it cannot be confined by outward form; it is only in the power of your own mind.

Go right ahead boldly and fiercely like a great warrior with a single sword mounted on a lone horse, plunging into a million-man army to kill the commander. That would be outstanding, would it not?

But if you think about whether it will be hard or easy, and worry about whether it is far or near, anxious about whether you will succeed or fail, then you cannot even stand on our own, let alone participate in Zen.

Yuan-hsien

True Mind

There are not many arts to Zen study: it just requires knowing your own true mind. Now observe that within this body the physical elements combine temporarily, daily heading for extinction: where is the true mind?

The flurry of ideas and thoughts arising and passing away without constancy is not the true mind.

That which shifts and changes unstably, sometimes good, sometimes bad, is not the true mind.

That which wholly depends on external things to manifest, and is not apparent when nothing is there, is not the true mind.

The heart inside the body cannot see itself, blind to the internal; it is not the true mind.

What is unaffected by feelings outside the body, cut off from the external, is not the true mind.

Suppose you turn the light of awareness around to look within, and sense a recondite tranquillity and calm oneness; do you consider this the true mind? You still do not realize that this recondite tranquillity and calm oneness are due to the perception of the false mind: there is the subjective mind perceiving and the object perceived — so this recondite tranquillity and calm oneness totally belong to the realm of inner states. This is what is meant by the *Heroic Progress Scripture* when it says, "Inwardly keeping to recondite tranquility is still a reflection of discrimination of objects." How could it be the true mind?

So if these are not the true mind, what is the true mind? Try to see what your true mind is, twenty-four hours a day. Don't try to figure it out, don't try to interpret it intellectually, don't try to get someone to explain it to you, don't seek some other technique, don't calculate how long it may take, don't calculate the degree of your own strength — just silently pursue this inner investigation on your own: "Ultimately what is my own true mind?"

Yuan-hsien

Empty and Quiet

People learning the way should first empty and quiet their minds. This is because the mind must be empty and quiet before it can mystically understand the subtle principle. If the mind is not emptied, it is like a pitcher full of donkey milk — how can you also fill it with lion milk? If the mind is not quiet, it is like a lamp in the wind, or like turbulent water — how can it reflect myriad forms?

Therefore learners should first stop cogitation and minimize objects of attention, making the mind empty and quiet. After that you have a basis for attaining the way. As Te-shan said, "Just have no mind on things and no things in your mind, and you will naturally be empty and spiritual, tranquil and sublime."

Nevertheless, you should not settle in empty quietude, sitting relaxed and untrammeled in nothingness. You must be truly attentive, investigating diligently, before you can break through the barrier of illusion and accomplish the great task. People's forces of habit, accumulated since beginningless time, are deep-seated; if you want to uproot them today, it will not be easy. You need to have a firm will constantly spurring you on. Strive to make progress in the work, without thinking about how much time it may take. When you have practiced for a long time, you will naturally become peaceful and whole. Why seek any other particular method?

Yuan-hsien

Avoiding Foxes and Dogs

The basic essential nature inherent in all people is clearly evident when you constantly perceive it within yourself; if you pursue external objects, then it becomes obscured; you get confused and are not awake.

That is why people of old would look into a saying — immediately attention is gathered on one point, and you are not drawn by the external world. Eventually the world is forgotten and objects disappear; then the original inherent light naturally comes through revealed.

If you arbitrarily start trying to figure the saying out, you immediately enter a mistaken path. If you want to ask other people, that too increases your confusion and distress. Therefore the method of looking into a saying is just to keep your mind on it, with a feeling of doubt that does not dissipate. Great doubt results in great enlightenment, small doubt results in small enlightenment, no doubt results in no enlightenment. This is an established fact.

People nowadays are unwilling to look into sayings: they just get together in groups to discuss this and that saying as being thus and so, calling it great enlightenment when they've managed to explain them clearly. Since the teachers have no true insight, when they see a resemblance in the words of others, they give them useless stamps of approval, saying they are people of attainment. The teachers and their followers are engaging in a mutual deception, defrauding each other.

That is why the way of Zen today has deteriorated and died out, while gangs of foxes and packs of dogs claim honor everywhere, fooling the whole world. They will go to hell like an arrow shot. If you want to study Zen, be sure not to fall into the company of those gangs of devils.

Yuan-hsien

List of Zen Masters

Fu Shan-hui (487–569)

Tao-hsin (580–651)

Niu-t'ou Hui-chung (683–769)

Ma-tsu (709–788)

Ta-chu (eighth century)

Ta-mei (ca. 805)

Pai-chang (720–814)

Tan-hsia (738–824)

Nan-ch'uan (747–834)

Kao-ch'eng (n.d.)

Te-shan (d. 867)

Ta-sui (800–880)

Ta-an (d. 883)

Tzu-hu (ninth century)

Yen-t'ou (827–887)

Chao-chou (778–897)

T'ou-tzu (845–914)

Lung-ya (834–920)

Hsuan-sha (ninth to tenth century)

Ku-shan (d. ca. 940)

Fa-yen (885–958)

Tung-shan Shou-ch'u (910/15–990/95)

Chih-men (fl. ca. 1000–1020)

Shih-shuang (986–1039)

She-hsien (tenth to eleventh century)

Sheng-ting (tenth to eleventh century)

Chieng-ku (fl. ca. 1037)

Yang-ch'i (992–1049)

Tao-wu Wu-chen (fl. ca. 1025–1060)

Fa-hua (fl. ca. 1000–1056)

Ta-yü Shou-chih (d. ca. 1060)

Tsu-hsin (eleventh century)

Ssu-hsin (eleventh century)

Chen-ching (exiled 1080)

Yun-feng Wen-yueh (d. ca. 1060)

I-ch'ing (1032–1083)

Hui-lin (1020–1099)

Fu-jung (1042–1118)

Huai-shan (fl. ca. 1115)

Hui-k'ung (1096–1158)

Tzu-te (1090–1159)

P'u-an (d. 1169)

Ying-an (d. 1163)

Huai-t'ang (twelfth century)

Fo-hsing T'ai (twelfth century)

Fu-an (twelfth century)

Yueh-lin (thirteenth century)

Sung-yuan (1140–1209)

P'o-an (1136–1211)

Ch'ih-chueh (fl. ca. 1208–1225)

Fo-chih (fl. ca. 1228)

Pei-chien (1185–1246)

Wu-chun (d. 1249)

Chueh-an (1250s)

Hsi-sou (fl. ca. 1249)

Yun-ku (fl. ca. 1256)

Wu-men (1183–1260)

Tuan-ch'iao (ca. 1241)

Hsueh-yen (fl. ca. 1253)

Hsi-yen (1198–1262)

Kao-feng (1260s)

Hsu-t'ang (1185–1269)

Hai-yin (ca. 1282)

Wu-chien (fl. ca. 1265–1300)

Ku-lin (fl. ca. 1297–1308)

Ming-pen (1263–1323)

Hsiao-yin (fl. ca. 1330)

Liao-an (fl. ca. 1330)

Wei-tse (d. 1348)

Shu-chung (d. 1386)

Nan-shih (fl. ca. 1368–1425)

Hui-ching (1528–1598)

Tzu-po (1543–1604)

Chien-ju (1549–1619)

Yuan-cheng (ca. 1570s–1620s)

Yuan-lai (1575–1630)

Ta-tu (seventeenth century)

Yuan-hsien (1618–1697)

Further Reading

Zen Essence: The Science of Freedom. Translated and edited by Thomas Cleary. Boston: Shambhala Publications, 1989.

Zen Lessons: The Art of Leadership. Translated by Thomas Cleary. Boston: Shambhala Publications, 1989.

Minding Mind: A Course in Basic Meditation. Translated by Thomas Cleary. Boston: Shambhala Publications, 1995.

Instant Zen: Waking Up in the Present. Translated by Thomas Cleary. Berkeley: North Atlantic Books, 1994.

Zen Letters: Teachings of Yuanwu. Translated by J.C. Cleary and Thomas Cleary. Boston: Shambhala Publications, 1994.

Buddhist Yoga: A Comprehensive Course. Translated by Thomas Cleary. Boston: Shambhala Publications, 1995.

The Observing Self: Mysticism and Psychotherapy. By Arthur J. Deikman, M.D. Boston: Beacon Press, 1982.